An Ou...
Royal ...

Hinterland

BY SEBASTIAN BARRY

WITHDRAWN
WRIGHT STATE UNIVERSITY LIBRARIES

This production was first performed at the
Octagon Theatre, Bolton on 17 January 2002

First performed in Ireland at the
Abbey Theatre Dublin on 30 January 2002

First performed in London at the
Royal National Theatre on 28 February 2002

PR
6052
.A729
H56
2002

Hinterland

TOUR DATES:

17 – 26 Jan
OCTAGON THEATRE, BOLTON
01204 520661

30 Jan – 23 Feb
ABBEY THEATRE, DUBLIN
00 353 1 878 7222
www.abbeytheatre.ie

28 Feb – 20 Apr
COTTESLOE,
ROYAL NATIONAL THEATRE
020 7452 3000
www.nationaltheatre.org.uk

23 – 27 Apr
ARTS THEATRE, CAMBRIDGE
01223 503333
www.cambridgeartstheatre.com

30 Apr – 4 May
THEATRE ROYAL BATH
01225 448844
www.theatreroyal.org.uk

6 May – 1 June
COTTESLOE,
ROYAL NATIONAL THEATRE
020 7452 3000
www.nationaltheatre.org.uk

4 – 8 June
OXFORD PLAYHOUSE
01865 305305
www.oxfordplayhouse.com

11 – 15 June
LIVERPOOL PLAYHOUSE
0151 709 4776
www.everymanplayhouse.co.uk

out of joint

Founded in 1993, Out of Joint is a national and international touring theatre company dedicated to the production of new writing. Under the direction of Max Stafford-Clark the company has premiered plays from leading writers including Sebastian Barry, Caryl Churchill, Mark Ravenhill and Timberlake Wertenbaker, as well as first-time writers like Simon Bennett.

"Britain's most successful touring company" THE STAGE

The Steward of Christendom

Touring all over the UK, Out of Joint frequently performs at and co-produces with key venues including Hampstead Theatre, the Liverpool Everyman & Playhouse, the Royal Court, the Royal National Theatre, Soho Theatre and the Young Vic. By co-producing its work the company is able to maintain a large on-going repertoire as well as premiering at least two new plays a year. Out of Joint is classed as one of the British Council's 'flagship' touring companies, with regular international tours to countries including India, Bulgaria, Russia, Egypt, Brazil, Australia, New Zealand, USA and many parts of Europe. Back home, Out of Joint also pursues an extensive education programme, with workshops in schools, universities and colleges and resource packs designed to accompany each production.

"Max Stafford-Clark's brilliant company" THE SCOTSMAN

The Positive Hour

Out of Joint's challenging and high-profile work has gained the company an international reputation and awards including the prestigious Prudential Award for Theatre. With a permanent commitment from the Arts Council of England, Out of Joint continues to commission, develop and produce new writing of the highest calibre.

"the excellent Out of Joint"
DAILY TELEGRAPH

Rita, Sue and Bob Too

out of joint

Director	Max Stafford-Clark
Producer	Graham Cowley
Marketing Manager	Alice Lascelles
Admin & Education Manager	Laura Collier
PA to Artistic Director & Assistant Director	Matthew Wilde
Literary Adviser	Ruth Little
Finance Officer	Sharon Smith
Writer in Residence	Mark Ravenhill

BOARD OF DIRECTORS

Kate Ashfield, Linda Bassett, John Blackmore (Chair), Elyse Dodgson, Sonia Friedman, Stephen Jeffreys, Paul Jesson, Karl Sydow

ARE YOU ON THE OJO MAILING LIST?

For information on upcoming shows, tour details and offers, send us your contact details, letting us know whether you'd like to receive information by post or email.

OJO EDUCATION WORK

Out of Joint offers a diverse programme of workshops and discussions for groups coming to see *Hinterland*. For more info on our 2002 education programme, resource packs, *Our Country's Good* and new writing workshops, contact Max or Laura at Out of Joint.

Post	7 Thane Works, Thane Villas, London N7 7PH
Phone	020 7609 0207
Fax	020 7609 0203
email	ojo@outofjoint.co.uk
Website	www.outofjoint.co.uk

Out of Joint is grateful to the following for their support over the years:

The Arts Council of England, The Foundation for Sport and the Arts, The Baring Foundation, The Paul Hamlyn Foundation, The Olivier Foundation, The Peggy Ramsay Foundation, The John S Cohen Foundation, The David Cohen Charitable Trust, The National Lottery through the Arts Council of England, The Prudential Awards, Stephen Evans, Karl Sydow, Harold Stokes and Friends of Theatre, John Lewis Partnership, Royal Victoria Hall Foundation.

Out of Joint is a registered charity no.1033059

THE ARTS COUNCIL OF ENGLAND

out of joint

PAST PRODUCTIONS & TOURS

2001

Sliding with Suzanne by Judy Upton
Feelgood by Alistair Beaton
• *Rita, Sue / A State Affair is revived for an international tour and Feelgood transfers to the West End, winning the Evening Standard award for Best Comedy.*

2000

Rita, Sue and Bob Too by Andrea Dunbar
& A State Affair by Robin Soans
• *Some Explicit Polaroids embarks on two more tours taking in America, France, Lithuania and Germany.*

1999

Some Explicit Polaroids by Mark Ravenhill
Drummers by Simon Bennett
• *Blue Heart has its New York premiere at BAM and Our Country's Good tours further to countries including Brazil, Israel, Bulgaria and Lithuania.*

1998

Our Country's Good by Timberlake Wertenbaker
Our Lady of Sligo by Sebastian Barry
• *Blue Heart is revived for a major international tour while Shopping and Fucking transfers to the West End, undertakes a further tour of the UK and receives its US premiere in New York.*

1997

Blue Heart by Caryl Churchill
The Positive Hour by April De Angelis
• *While Shopping and Fucking begins its first UK tour, Steward of Christendom follows on from its success of the previous two years with an appearance at BAM in New York.*

1996

Shopping and Fucking by Mark Ravenhill
• *Three Sisters and Break of Day is revived for a tour of India and a run at the Lyric, Hammersmith, while The Steward of Christendom and The Queen and I embark on Australian tours in quick succession.*

1995

The Steward of Christendom by Sebastian Barry
Three Sisters by Anton Chekhov
& Break of Day by Timberlake Wertenbaker
• *The Queen and I begins a second UK tour while The Man of Mode and The Libertine conclude a national tour with a run at the Royal Court.*

1994

The Man of Mode by George Etherege &
The Libertine by Stephen Jeffreys
The Queen and I by Sue Townsend & Road by Jim Cartwright
• *Out of Joint is launched with two double-bills, both of which go on to extensive UK tours.*

The National Theatre

The Abbey and Peacock Theatres

The name Abbey Theatre is popularly applied throughout the world to all aspects of what is, in fact the National Theatre of Ireland. From its inception in 1904 to the present day, writers and theatre artists remain at the centre of the Abbey Theatre policies which have helped to establish it as one of Ireland's foremost cultural institutions.

The Abbey Theatre today

Under the current artistic direction of Ben Barnes, the National Theatre aims to promote and develop new Irish plays, revitalise and present plays from the Irish repertoire as well as classics of the European and World stages.

The Abbey Theatre has a long history of touring abroad - last year our productions were seen as far away as California and Singapore. This year **Translations** by Brian Friel toured to the International Festival of Arts and Ideas in Connecticut and visited a number of venues across Europe, from Teatre Nacional de Catalunya in Barcelona to the Vigszinhaz Theatre, Budapest.

The old Abbey Theatre

The Abbey Theatre continues to attract critical acclaim at home and abroad. It was the recipient of eight Irish Times/ESB Awards, including that of Best Theatre Company for its work in 2000 which included the Warner/Shaw production of **Medea** and the controversial production of **Barbaric Comedies**. The work of the Abbey Theatre has been recognised in the Evening Standard Awards and the Olivier Awards in 2001 and looks forward to touring its highly regarded retrospective of the work of Tom Murphy and **Medea** in 2002.

Fiona Shaw in **Medea** by Euripides, translated by Kenneth McLeish and Frederic Raphael photo: Neil Libbert

Don Wycherley in **Eden**
by Eugene O'Brien
Photo: Paul McCarthy

Eamon Morrissey in
Barbaric Comedies
by Ramon Maria del Valle-Inclan in a
new version by Frank McGuinness
Photo: Douglas Robertson

Fidelma Keogh and Barry Barnes in
Translations by Brian Friel
Photo: Paul McCarthy

Sebastian Barry has had a long and fruitful relationship with the Abbey Theatre who premiered his first play, **Boss Grady's Boys**. In 1990 he was Ansbacher Writer-in-Association at the Abbey Theatre where **Prayers of Sherkin** was produced. **White Woman Street** transferred to the Peacock Theatre after a run at the Bush Theatre in London and in 1995 for the Dublin Theatre Festival, **The Only True History of Lizzie Finn** was premiered on the main stage. It is therefore with great pleasure that we welcome **Hinterland**, Sebastian's latest play, to the Abbey Theatre.

Alongside the productions in the Abbey and Peacock Theatres, there is a full programme of work from the Literary Department and Archive and the Outreach/Education Department ensuring that the work of the National Theatre is enjoyed by as wide an audience as possible.

The Abbey Theatre is principally funded by the Arts Council of Ireland/An Chomhairle Ealaíon but we would also like to gratefully acknowledge the financial support of the British Council who are generously supporting this production of **Hinterland** in Dublin.

For further information on The Abbey Theatre and its productions, please call our box office 00 353 1 878 7222 or check out the website at www.abbeytheatre.ie

The Arts Council
An Chomhairle Ealaíon

The
British
Council

ABBEY THEATRE DUBLIN

Board
James Hickey
(Chairman)
Bernard Farrell
Eithne Healy
Jennifer Johnston
John McColgan
Pauline Morrison
Niall O'Brien
Deirdre Purcell
Michael J. Somers

Artistic Director
Ben Barnes

Managing Director
Richard Wakely

General Manager
Martin Fahy

Director's Office
Ciara Flynn
(P.A. Artistic Director)
Grainne Howe
(P.A. Secretary)

Associate Directors
Garry Hynes
Laszlo Marton
Paul Mercier
Katie Mitchell
Conall Morrison
Lynne Parker
Deborah Warner

**Honorary Associate
Directors**
Vincent Dowling
Tomas MacAnna

Abbey Players
Clive Geraghty
Des Cave

Staff Director
David Parnell

Casting Director
Marie Kelly

Voice Coach
Andrea Ainsworth

**Writer-In-
Association**
sponsored by
Anglo Irish Bank
Jim Nolan

Archive
Mairead Delaney
(Archivist)

Box Office
Adam Lawlor
(Box Office Manager)
Des Byrne
(Box Office Assistant)
Clare Downey
(Chief Cashier)

Box Office Clerks
Catherine Casey
Anne Marie Doyle
Edel Hanly
Lorraine Hanna
Maureen Robertson
David Windrim

Front of House
Pauline Morrison
(House Manager)
John Baynes
(Deputy House Manager)

Cleaning
Joe McNamara
(Supervisor)

Reception
Niamh Douglas
(Senior Receptionist)
Sandra Williams
(Receptionist)

Stage Door
Patrick Gannon
Patrick Whelan

Ushers
Jim O'Keeffe
(Chief Usher)
Daniel Byrne
Ruth Colgan
Con Doyle
Ivan Kavanagh
Simon Lawlor
Seamus Mallin
Fred Murray

Education
Sharon Murphy
(Head of Outreach/
Education)
Sarah Jordan
(Administrator)
Jean O'Dwyer
(Projects Officer)
Joanna Parkes
(Projects Officer)

Finance
Margaret Bradley
(Financial Controller)
Margaret Flynn
(Accounts)
Pat O'Connell
(Payroll)

Literary
Judy Friel
(Literary Mgr.)
Jocelyn Clarke
(Commissioning Mgr.)
Orla Flanagan
(Literary Officer)

**Press and
Marketing**
Press
Representation
Kate Bowe PR
Katherine
Brownridge
(Marketing Manager)
Tina Connell
(Promotions Officer)
Lucy McKeever
(Press & Programmes
Officer)

Technical
Tony Wakefield
(Technical Director)
Tommy Nolan
(Production Manager)
Peter Rose
(Construction Manager)
Vanessa Fitz-Simon
(Asst. Production
Manager)

Carpenters
Mark Joseph Darley
(Master Carpenter)
John Kavanagh
(Deputy)
Brian Comiskey
Bart OFarrell
Kenneth Crowe
(Assistant)

Scenic Artists
Angie Benner
Jennifer Moonan

Design
Emma Cullen
(Design Assistant)

Electricians
Mick Doyle
(Chief Electrician)
Brian Fairbrother
Joe Glasgow
Barry Madden
Kevin McFadden
(Acting Deputy)

**Information
Technology**
Dave OBrien
(Manager)

Maintenance
Brian Fennell
(Maintenance Engineer)
Tony Delaney
(Assistant)

Props
Stephen Molloy
(Property Master)

Stage Managers
John Andrews
Gerry Doyle

Stage Hands
Aaron Clear
Mick Doyle
(Fly Master)
Pat Dillon
Paul Kelly

Stage Directors
Finola Eustace
(Head of Department)
John Stapleton
Audrey Hession

**Assistant Stage
Managers**
Stephen Dempsey
Maree Kearns

Sound
Dave Nolan
(Chief Sound Technician)
Cormac Carroll
Nuala Golden

Wardrobe
Joan OClery
(Acting Wardrobe
Supervisor)
Fiona Talbot
(Acting Deputy)
Angela Hanna
Vicky Miller
Catherine Fay
Frances Kelly
(Wigs & Hairdressing)
Patsy Giles
(Make-Up)

Royal National Theatre
South Bank, London SE1 9PX

Hinterland is a co-production between the National Theatre, Abbey Theatre Dublin and Out of Joint. The production plays in repertory in the Cottesloe Theatre at the National from February to May 2002. Within the National are three separate theatres, the Olivier, the Lyttelton, and the Cottesloe.

The chief aims of the National, under the direction of Trevor Nunn, are to present a diverse repertoire, embracing classic, new and neglected plays; to present these plays to the very highest standards; and to give audiences a wide choice.

We offer all kinds of other events and services - short early-evening platform performances; work for children and education work; free live entertainment both inside and outdoors at holiday times; exhibitions; live foyer music; backstage tours; bookshops; plenty of places to eat and drink; and easy car-parking. And the nearby Studio acts as a resource for research and development for actors, writers and directors.

We send productions on tour, both in this country and abroad, and do all we can, through ticket-pricing, to make the NT accessible to everyone regardless of income.

The National Theatre was founded in 1963, with Laurence Olivier as Director. For its first years, the Company worked at the Old Vic Theatre, while waiting for the new building on the South Bank of the Thames to be completed. In 1976, under Peter Hall, the move took place. Since its inception, the National has presented nearly 500 plays, and at least five different productions are presented in its three theatres in any one week. Richard Eyre was Director of the Royal National Theatre from 1988 until 1997, when he was succeeded by Trevor Nunn. Nicholas Hytner will become the National's Director in April 2003.

Box Office: 020 7452 3000

Chairman of the Board
Sir Christopher Hogg
Director of the Royal National Theatre
Trevor Nunn
Director Designate
Nicholas Hytner
Executive Director
Genista McIntosh
Head of Touring
Roger Chapman

Funded by the Arts Council of England
Registered Charity No. 224223

An Out of Joint, Abbey Theatre Dublin,
Royal National Theatre co-production

Hinterland

by Sebastian Barry

Cast in order of appearance:

Patrick Malahide	Johnny Silvester
James Hayes	Stephen
Kieran Ahern	Cornelius
Dearbhla Molloy	Daisy
Phelim Drew	Jack
Lucianne McEvoy	Aisling
Anna Healy	Connie

Director	Max Stafford-Clark
Designer	Es Devlin
Lighting	Johanna Town
Sound	Paul Arditti
Music	Paddy Cunneen
Company & Stage Manager	Christine Hathway
Deputy Stage Manager	Sally McKenna
Assistant Stage Manager	Leila Jones
Production Manager	Sacha Milroy for Background
Assistant Director	Matthew Wilde
Costume Supervisor	Fizz Jones
Production Electrician	Tim Bray
Casting Director	Serena Hill
Fight Director	Terry King
Production and Poster Photography	John Haynes
Poster Design	Iain Lanyon

For Out of Joint:

Producer	Graham Cowley
Marketing Manager	Alice Lascelles
Administration & Education Manager	Laura Collier

Production credits:
Habitat
Service Point Reprographics
Sambataro, Stables Market, Camden
Roger & Sheida Jones
Any Amount of Books, 56 Charing Cross Road
Bush plc
Paperchase
Bang & Olufsen

With thanks to:
National Theatre Furniture Hire Dept
Jane Slattery

Sebastian Barry (Writer)

Born in 1955 in Dublin and educated at the Catholic University School and Trinity College, Dublin. Published a number of books of poetry and prose until 1988, when his first play, *Boss Grady's Boys*, was produced at the Abbey Theatre in Dublin. Since then five further plays have appeared, including *Prayers of Sherkin* and two Out of Joint productions, *Steward of Christendom* and *Our Lady of Sligo*, both directed by Max Stafford-Clark. His novel *The Whereabouts of Eneas McNulty* was published in 1998. His new novel *Annie Dunne* will be published in 2002 by Faber & Faber. He lives in Wicklow with his wife Alison and three children, Merlin, Coral and Tobias.

Paul Arditti (Sound)

Paul Arditti has been designing sound for theatre since 1983. He currently combines his post as Head of Sound at the Royal Court (where he has designed more than 60 productions) with regular freelance projects. Royal Court includes: *Boy Gets Girl, Clubland, Far Away, Mouth to Mouth, 4:48 Psychosis, Blasted, Spinning Into Butter, The Glory of Living, I Just Stopped By To See The Man, My Zinc Bed, The Force of Change, Dublin Carol, The Kitchen, Rat in the Skull, Some Voices, Mojo, The Weir, Via Dolorosa, Hysteria; The Chairs* (co-production with Complicite – Drama Desk nomination in New York). Out of Joint includes: *The Steward of Christendom, Shopping and Fucking, Blue Heart, Sliding With Suzanne* (with Royal Court); *Our Lady of Sligo* (with RNT); *Some Explicit Polaroids*. Other theatre includes: *Afore Night Come* (Young Vic); *Tales From Hollywood* (Donmar); *Light* (Complicite); *Hamlet, The Tempest* (RSC); *Orpheus Descending* (West End & Broadway); *Cyrano de Bergerac* (West End); *St Joan* (West End & Australia); *Marathon* (Gate London). Musicals include: *Doctor Dolittle* (West End), *Piaf* (West End), *The Threepenny Opera* (Donmar). Awards include: Drama Desk Award for Outstanding Sound Design 1992 for *Four Baboons Adoring the Sun* (Broadway).

Paddy Cunneen (Music)

Paddy Cunneen has worked extensively as a composer and music director in theatre throughout the UK and Ireland. His work runs to well over 100 productions for the RNT, RSC, Cheek By Jowl, Donmar Warehouse, Abbey, Gate and Druid Theatres, Manchester Royal Exchange, Royal Court, Liverpool Everyman and many others. In addition he composes for BBC Radio Drama, RTE Radio Drama and has a number of TV and film credits. He is a recipient of the Christopher Whelen Award for Music in Theatre.

Graham Cowley (Producer)

Out of Joint's Producer since 1998. His long collaboration with Max Stafford-Clark began as Joint Stock Theatre Group's first General Manager for seven years in the 1970s. He was General Manager of the Royal Court for eight years, and on their behalf transferred a string of hit plays to the West End. His career has spanned the full range of theatre production, from small fringe companies to major West End shows and large scale commercial tours. Most recently transferred the Royal Court's production of *The Weir* to the West End, produced *A Kind of Alaska* at the Edinburgh Festival and in the USA, and *Harry and Me* at the Warehouse Theatre, Croydon.

Es Devlin (Designer)

Trained at Bristol University, Central Saint Martins and Motley Theatre Design Course. **Theatre** designs include: *A Day in the Death of Joe Egg* (New Ambassadors); *The Prisoner's Dilemma* (RSC); *Meat* (Theatre Royal, Plymouth, Nominated for TMA 2001 Best Design Award); *Howie the Rookie* (Bush Theatre, Winner of TMA 1999 Best Design Award); *Henry IV* (RSC); *Betrayal* (RNT); *Rita, Sue and Bob Too / A State Affair* (Out of Joint/Soho Theatre); *Hamlet* (Young Vic, Tokyo Globe); *Credible Witness, Yard Gal* (Royal Court); *Snake in the Grass* (Old Vic); *Piano* (TPT Tokyo); *Love and Understanding, Love You Too, One Life and Counting, Drink, Dance, Laugh, Lie* (Bush Theatre); *Perapalas* (Gate Theatre); *The Death of Cool* (Hampstead Theatre); *Closer to Heaven* (Arts Theatre); *Edward II* (Bolton Octagon, Winner of the 1995 Linbury Prize for Stage Design). **Opera** designs include: *Hansel and Gretel* (Scottish Opera Go Round); *Fidelio* (English Touring Opera); *Powder Her Face* (Ystad Festival, Sweden); *Don Giovanni* (British Youth Opera). Designs for **dance** include: *A Streetcar Named Desire* (Northern Ballet Theatre); *God's Plenty* and *Four Scenes* both for Rambert Dance Company. Designs for **film** include: *Brilliant!* (Ten by Ten for BBC2); *A Tale of Two Heads, Beggars Belief, Snow on Saturday* (winner of the Kino Best British Short Film 2001).

Max Stafford-Clark (Director)

Founded Joint Stock Theatre Group in 1974 following his Artistic Directorship of The Traverse Theatre, Edinburgh. From 1979 to 1993 he was Artistic Director of the Royal Court. In 1993 he founded Out of Joint. His work as a director has overwhelmingly been with new writing and he has commissioned and directed first productions by many of the country's leading writers.

Johanna Town (Lighting)

Johanna Town has been Head of Lighting at the Royal Court Theatre, London for the past ten years and has designed extensively for the company over that period. **Theatre** productions include: The *Kitchen, Faith Healer, Pale Horse, Search and Destroy, Women Laughing* and most recently *Fucking Games, Nightingale & Chase, I Just Stopped By To See the Man, Spinning into Butter, Mr Kolpert* and *Under The Blue Sky. Hinterland* is Johanna's 11th production for Out of Joint, past productions include: *Rita, Sue and Bob Too / A State Affair, The Steward of Christendom, Shopping & Fucking, Our Lady of Sligo, Blue Heart* and *Feelgood*. Further theatre credits include: *Les Liasons Dangereuses* (Liverpool Playhouse), *Top Girls* (Oxford Stage Co / Savoy West End), *Playboy of the Western World* (Liverpool Playhouse), Arabian Nights (New Victory, New York), *Ghosts* (Royal Exchange Theatre), *Rose* (Lyceum Theatre, New York), *Little Malcolm and His Struggle Against the Eunuchs* (West End), *Some Explicit Polaroids* (Out of Joint, World Tour). **Opera** credits include: *Tobias & the Angel* (Almeida Opera festival), *La Boheme, Die Fledermaus, La Traviata,* (Music Theatre London), *Abduction from Seraglio, Marriage of Figaro* (Opera 80), *Marriage of Figaro, Otello* (Opera du Nice, France).

Matthew Wilde (Assistant Director)

Trained and studied at Bretton Hall, RADA & Kings College, London. As assistant director: *Camino Real, Twelfth Night, Sweet Bird of Youth* and *The Honest Whore* (RADA). As director theatre includes: *The Insatiate Countess* (Young Vic Studio Workshop), *Women Beware Women, Prometheus In Evin* and *Brighton Beach Scumbags* (Brockley Jack Theatre), *Romeo and Juliet, Macbeth* (Southwark Playhouse), *The Crucible* and *Vinegar Tom* (RADA at The Old Vic) and *Paradise* (Moray House Theatre, Edinburgh). Matthew is the Artistic Director of electric storm productions and is involved in developing and presenting new writing with writers from the Royal Court YWP, Goldsmith's College and RADA. He is also a member of the Readers' Panel at Soho Theatre and has worked extensively on various young people's theatre projects both in London and nationally, most recently with the English Shakespeare Company.

Kieran Ahern (*Cornelius*)

Kieran has worked extensively both nationally and internationally throughout his career to date. **Theatre** highlights include the role of Smith in the original cast of Sebastian Barry's *The Steward of Christendom* (Out of Joint/Royal Court) directed by Max Stafford Clark, which played in London, Dublin, Luxembourg, Sydney, Wellington and New York. In 1997 he originated the role of Jim in Conor McPherson's award-winning play *The Weir* (Royal Court) directed by Ian Rickson. The production toured extensively playing London, Dublin, Brussels, Toronto and Broadway. Recently Kieran played Isaac Dunn in the premiere of Marina Carr's *On Raftery's Hill* (Druid/Royal Court) directed by Gary Hynes, playing in Galway, Dublin, London and Washington. Most recently he played Akaki in Johnny Hanrahan's adapation of Dostoyevsky's short story *The Overcoat* (Meridian) at the Dublin Theatre Festival 2001. Other theatre includes *Tartuffe* (Gate Theatre); *Normal* (Meridian); *The Illusion* (Charabanc); *Lady Windermere's Fan* (Rough Magic). **Film/Television**: *The Last September*, *Titanic Town*, *The Matchmaker*, *Meteor*, *Love and Rage*, *Before I Sleep*, *Inspector Morse*, *Amongst Women*, *The Governor*, *Amazing Love Stories*, *Edward No Hands*, *The Widow's Son*, *White*.

Phelim Drew (*Jack*)

Theatre includes: *Whistle in the Dark*, *The Wake*, *The Rivals*, *The Playboy of the Western World*, *The Corsican Brothers*, *The Plough and the Stars* all for the Abbey Theatre, Dublin; *Therese Raquin*, *Christmas Carol*, *Weeping of Angels*, *She Stoops to Conquer*, *Pride and Prejudice*, *Present Laughter*, *Moonlight*, *The Double Dealer*, *Tartuffe* (Gate Theatre, Dublin); *Judas* (Kilkenny Theatre); *The Plough and the Stars*, *John Bull's Other Island*, *Borstal Boy* (Gaiety Theatre); *Rough for Theatre I* and *II* (Beckett Festival, Gate); *Brothers of the Brush* (Arts Theatre, London); *Galileo* (Almeida); *The Dream*, *The Recruiting Officer* (Lyceum Theatre, Edinburgh); *Love and a Bottle* (Rough Magic); *Cheapside* (Druid); *Danny, the Witch and the Goblin*, *Prayers of Sherkin*, *Blinded by the Light* (Peacock Theatre); *Spenser's Laye* (Smock Alley, The Project); *As you Like It* (The Tivoli); *Red Noses* (Pigsback); *Breaking Up* (Passion Machine). **Film** includes: *The Escapist* (Escapist Films); *Kaos* (Amox Ltd); *Angela's Ashes* (Universal); *Old New Borrowed Blue* (Revolution Films); *Shergar* (Blue Rider Pictures); *The Nephew* (World 2000); *The Commitments* (Beacon / First Film / Dirty Hands); *My Left Foot* (Palace). **Television** includes: *Making the Cut* (RTE); *Mirad A Boy From Bosnia* (Double Exposure); *Sharpe's Battle* (Sharpe Films) and *The Ambassador*.

James Hayes (*Stephen*)

Trained at the Guildhall School of Music and Drama. Recent **theatre**: *The Relapse* (National Theatre), *Belonging* (Birmingham Rep), *Hamlet* and *The Antipodes* (Shakespeare's Globe), *Richard II, As You Like It, The White Devil, The Good Natured Man, Macbeth, The Front Page, The Misanthrope, Grand Manoeuvres* (National Theatre at the Old Vic), *Galileo, The Romans in Britain, Amadeus, Strider, The Spanish Tragedy, As I Lay Dying, Coriolanus, The Fawn, The Oresteia, A Chorus Of Disapproval, A View From The Bridge, Othello* and two one man shows, *A Horde Of Unemployed, Ventriloquists* and *Russell Of The Times* (National Theatre), *The Tempest, Elgar's Rondo, The Venetian Twins, The Hostage, The Taming Of The Shrew, Faust, Woyzeck, The Cherry Orchard, The Lion The Witch and The Wardrobe, The Winter's Tale* (Royal Shakespeare Company). Other work in London: *Faith, Hope And Charity* (Lyric Hammersmith) *The Beaux, Stratagem* (Cambridge Theatre) *The Rules Of The Game* (Albery) *A View From The Bridge* (Aldwych) *Lenny* (Queens). Recent **TV**: *A Touch Of Frost, Leprechauns, The Winters Tale. Waking The Dead, The Jury, Playing The Field.* Recent **Radio**: Wrote and performed in *Picture This* and *The Burning Of Bridget Cleary* for RTE.

Anna Healy (*Connie*)

Theatre credits include: *The Hunt for Red Willie, Mrs Warren's Profession, Dancing at Lughnasa, The Electrocution of Children, The Wake, The Marriage of Figaro* all for the Abbey Theatre, Dublin; *Oliver Twist, The Breadman, Jane Eyre, Threepenny Opera, The Cherry Orchard* (Gate Theatre, Dublin); *Eddie Bottom's Dream* (Double Joint, Dublin); *Shadow of a Gunman* (Citizens, Glasgow); *Tulip Futures* (Cockpit Theatre); *Bohemian Lights, Hecuba, The Cheating Hearts* (Gate Theatre, London); *Long Days Journey Into Night* (Cambridge Theatre Co.); *Peer Gynt, Abingdon Square* (National Theatre); *Victory, Culture Vultures, A Little Night Music* (Chichester Festival). **Film** and **television** includes: *Fergus's Wedding* (Grand Pictures), *Cause of Death* (McGuffin Films/BBC); *Cardiac Arrest* (BBC); *Ladybird, Ladybird* (Parallax); *Orlando* (Adventure Pictures); *Madly in Love* (Channel Four); *Easter Saturday* (Yellow Asylum Films – winner of the Dublin City Arts Council Prize and award at the Cork Film Festival); *The Bomb – One Year On* (ITV). **Radio** includes: *Firefly Summer, The Last September, One Winter by the Foyle, The Absentee* (Radio 4); *Maiden City Magic* (Radio Ulster); *The Cure at Troy* (BBC Radio 3).

Patrick Malahide (*Johnny Silvester*)

Born in England of Irish parents. Educated at Douai School and Edinburgh University. **Theatre** includes: *Mutabilitie* (Royal National Theatre); *Map of the Heart* (Globe); *Operation Bad Apple* (Royal Court); *In the Ruins* (Royal Court / Bristol Old Vic); *Uncle Vanya, Clandestine Marriage, The Cherry Orchard, Accidental Death of an Anarchist, King Lear, The Tempest* (Bristol Old Vic); *Cockups* (Royal Exchange); *Judgement* (Liverpool Playhouse/Dublin Theatre Festival); *Every Good Boy Deserves Favour* (Traverse Theatre); *The Android Circuit* (Traverse Theatre/ICA); *The Crucible* (Birmingham Rep); *Major Barbara, Two Gentlemen of Verona, The Homecoming, Look Back in Anger, Endgame* (Royal Lyceum, Edinburgh). **Film** includes: *Captain Corelli's Mandolin, Billy Elliot, The World Is Not Enough, Ordinary Decent Criminal, US Marshals, The Beautician and the Beast, The Long Kiss Goodnight, Cutthroat Island, Two Deaths, A Man Of No Importance, December Bride, A Month In The Country, Comfort and Joy, The Killing Fields*. **Television** includes: *Victoria and Albert; All The King's Men, Deacon Brodie, Middlemarch, The Inspector Alleyn Mysteries, Who Bombed Birmingham?, Children of the North, The Franchise Affair, Miss Julie, The Singing Detective, The Russian Soldier, Pity in History, The Pickwick Papers, Video Stars, Black Adder, The Standard, Inspector Morse, The One Game, Charlie, After the War* and five series of *Minder*.

Lucianne McEvoy (*Aisling*)

Lucianne graduated from the Samuel Beckett Centre, Trinity College and was awarded a distinction for her work there. During that time **theatre** work included: Bríd O Milleáin in *The Artaud Project* directed by Michael Bogdanov; First God in *The Good Person of Szechuan* directed by Lily Todd; Mary Brenham in *Our Country's Good* directed by Jason Byrne. Since then, she has played Anna Owens in *Dolly West's Kitchen* directed by Patrick Mason at the Abbey and the Old Vic; Bridget in *Translations* directed by Ben Barnes for the Abbey and European Tour; Annas in the Irish premiere of Frank McGuinness' *Mutabilitie* directed by Michael Caven for Theatreworks. **Film** roles include Máire in *A Family Affair* (UCD) and Mary in *The Pear Bottle* (Igloo Productions). **Radio** work includes *If I Could Fly* and *Stardust* (RTE).

Dearbhla Molloy (*Daisy*)

Most recent **theatre** credits include *Juno and the Paycock* (Donmar Warehouse); *Saturday, Sunday, Monday* (Chichester Festival Theatre); *Experiment with an Air Pump* (Manchester Royal Exchange); *The Cripple of Inishmaan* and *On the Ledge* (RNT); *Arcadia* (Haymarket Theatre); *The Hostage* (RSC), and a just-finished premiere of Conor McPherson's *Come on Over* at the Gate Theatre, Dublin. Theatre in the US includes: *Dancing at Lughnasa* (Broadway, Tony Award nomination), *Juno and the Paycock* (Roundabout at the Gramercy); *The Cripple of Inishmaan* (Geffen Playhouse, Los Angeles) and *Touch of the Poet* (ART Boston). **TV and film** include: *Breur* (Disney/Fox) and *Outreach* (Warner). Recent TV in Britain includes *Swallow, The Fragile Heart, GBH, Romeo and Juliet* and the recently filmed *Fergus' Wedding* comedy series, to be screened in Spring. Film includes: *This is the Sea, Frankie Starlight, Run of the Country, Laded, Taffin, Bug.*

Sebastian Barry
Hinterland

faber and faber

First published in 2002
by Faber and Faber Limited
3 Queen Square, London WC1N 3AU
Published in the United States by Faber and Faber Inc.
an affiliate of Farrar, Straus and Giroux LLC, New York

Typeset by Country Setting, Kingsdown, Kent CT14 8ES
Printed in England by Mackays of Chatham plc, Chatham, Kent

All rights reserved

Copyright © Sebastian Barry, 2002

The right of Sebastian Barry to be identified as author
of this work has been asserted in accordance with
Section 77 of the Copyright, Designs and Patents Act 1988

All rights whatsoever in this work are strictly reserved.
Applications for permission for any use whatsoever
including performance rights must be made in advance, prior
to any such proposed use, to The Agency, 24 Pottery Lane,
Holland Park, London W11 4LZ. No performance
may be given unless a licence has first been obtained

*This book is sold subject to the condition that it shall not, by
way of trade or otherwise, be lent, resold, hired out or otherwise
circulated without the publisher's prior consent in any form of
binding or cover other than that in which it is published and
without a similar condition including this condition being
imposed on the subsequent purchaser*

A CIP record for this book
is available from the British Library

ISBN 0–571–21003–1

2 4 6 8 10 9 7 5 3 1

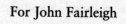
For John Fairleigh

Characters

Johnny
Daisy
Jack
Stephen
Cornelius
Aisling
Connie

Act One

The private study in a Georgian mansion, outside Dublin, present day. All the paraphernalia of a successful political life – citations, presentations, election posters framed. Many books, and the walls enduring a storm of modern Irish paintings, Le Broquy, O'Malley et cetera.

Two Georgian windows look out on to an arrangement of formal gardens, box-wood and avenues fleeting in the distance.

It is early winter evening, the rain cascades silently beyond the glass. Johnny Silvester, a man of seventy years, finely dressed to the point of mummified dandyism, sits alone writing at the centre of the table, a little expensive reading lamp near his pages.

A radio plays softly on the desk.

No lights have been turned on as yet. He pulls the brittle green shade closer and clicks on the light, looks back at the growing dark, continues to write.

Johnny (*reading back over what he has written*) 'And it has been on my mind recently to write to you both, my dear aunts, in Derry, where so many of my childhood memories reside. My mind often returns to the poignant fact that Derry was once the market town for a much greater district, before partition divided the old city from her own hinterland of Donegal. How often my father and his brothers remarked that the border did not only separate farmer from market, pig from pen, cow from herd, as you might say, but also heart from heartland, and indeed, as in our case, father from fatherland. Because my father was hardly the same man after partition, and his physical breakdown may well have been hastened by the same imposition, an eventuality of course that he strove to prevent by every means, and which I myself while in office often . . . ' (*in mild despair*) Stilted and formal. I have got to get the historical angle out of my mind. To think Seamus Heaney turned his Derry childhood into the stuff of a Nobel Prize. This bloody thing sounds like a court affidavit. Loosen up, Johnny. You're writing to your two old aunts, not the Attorney-General. (*He scrunches up the paper.*) It's at times like this that a person might want to talk to his wife. But I mustn't do that. It would be moral weakness of the highest order.

A knock on the door and a man in his seventies enters with a silver tray.

Johnny Leave it at my side, Stephen, I'm in midstream here.

Stephen I won't disturb you, Mr Silvester.

Johnny Well, and you never do.

Stephen sets down the tray. He makes to go but Johnny stops him after all.

How is everything about the house this winter evening of our lives, as the poet said?

Stephen I heard her up in her room crying, sir.

Johnny I was hoping all that had passed. That crying. Wherefore crying, Stephen? Moral, maybe. It is moral crying, the worst, the most afflicting.

Stephen I knocked to see if she was alright.

Johnny And she said something?

Stephen She came out and said she was going down to the drawing room to dust the porcelain.

Johnny That's the old routine, alas. Just yesterday we heard, it will all start again in the spring – my sweet

8

interrogation at the hands of the nation. But better days ahead, Stephen. Time will indeed dry those tears. The circle will get wider and wider until – happiness. Because I will keep firm, keep fast. I will – demonstrate – with demonstrations of . . .

Stephen A man must do right by his own people.

Johnny Of course, of course. I think I follow you, Stephen.

Sound of car coming down the drive, headlights flaring in the window.

Stephen To-ing and fro-ing.

Johnny Used to be more of it. Who is it?

Stephen Special Branch man, returning from his afternoon pint at the pub.

Johnny He's supposed to be guarding us around the clock. How do you know, Stephen?

Stephen Ford Cortina, 1978. Engine noises are a hobby of mine. I have a gift for it.

Johnny Poor bastard.

Stephen surprised.

The Special Branch man, I mean. An old banger like that.

Stephen Oh, no, Mr Silvester. He has it fully restored. Collector's item. He is a – beatnik. On his day off. So he tells me.

Johnny Beatniks are extinct.

Stephen There's little sign of intelligent life in him, right enough. A rum character. I see him talking at the gates with curious onlookers and journalists. He's up and down the cinder path like a flame on a fender.

Johnny He is discouraging them, I hope.

Stephen Is he going to roost with us here for ever, undesired and, I'm afraid, largely unwashed?

Johnny Not undesired, Stephen. Someone to watch over us.

Stephen Do you fancy anything else, sir?

Johnny No, that's grand now. The tea will sort me out. (*A moment.*) Time will dry those tears, I am sure.

Stephen That's how it works. (*just as he is going*) How did you get on with the doctor this morning?

Johnny He has left me with a slightly unpleasant feeling in my rear-end, to tell you the truth.

Stephen He was encouraging?

Johnny A urologist is a cross between a plumber and an antique dealer. Assessing old fixtures. He did a what's-it, took a thingummy.

Stephen A sample?

Johnny I'm not a carpet.

Stephen A urine sample, I meant, sir.

Johnny Oh, yes, one of those, excuse me. But that was only the warmer-upper. Then he did the what's-it, kind of cutting a bit off, or scraping just maybe, or swabbing did he call it, did it in his rooms, which really took me aback. It's no joke bending over in a man's offices, looking at the pencil holders on his desk and the mechanical calendar. He's going to ring me.

Stephen Oh, I know what he did. An autopsy.

Johnny I'm not dead yet, Stephen.

Stephen Ah, biopsy. That's it. So, well, we'll be fully informed in due course then, sir?

Johnny We will.

Stephen Well, goodnight, sir. (*Goes.*)

Johnny Goodnight. (*After a little breathes deeply, into the stomach. Counts three silently. Releases the breath.*) Not quite the retirement I had in mind. But so is it given to many men. I have done the state some service, but enough of . . . (*The phone rings.*) Is that you, Doctor? (*He lifts it.*) Yes? Hello? What? How did you get this number? No! (*Slams down phone.*) Fucking journalists! (*Leaps up, paces.*) How could she ask me such a question? Dying? What a question! Are you dying, Mr Silvester? Cunt! (*Sits into his easy chair, breathes out. Slowly his face settles into a stare. He puts his hands over his face slowly.*) Oh, Christ. Christ. (*after a moment*) An aged man is but a paltry thing, a tattered coat upon a, something – stick maybe. Yeats. Christ! Dignity. That's the key. Be dignified. I will not dignify that question with an answer, I ought to have said. Calm, peaceful, with dignity. A nap. And awake refreshed. Lovely that would be. Awake and it is no longer true. Long life, prosperity. An old statesman in his well-earned retirement. Dignity. (*Drops into a doze.*)

A sound as if someone were turning the tuning dial of the radio. Cornelius, jovial and robust, in his early sixties, comes in mysteriously through an open cupboard – it is a cupboard half cleared out, deep and large, with some official-looking piles of paper still in it. Cornelius raises his arms and sings:

Cornelius
    'Oh, rise up, lovely Sweeney, and give your horse
      some hay.

And give him out a feed of oats before you start
    the day.
Don't feed him rocks of turnips, take him down to
    yon great lawn.
And there he will be able . . .

Together
    . . . for to plough the rocks of Bawn!'

Johnny Cornelius! Cornelius!

Cornelius How are ya, Johnny?

Johnny rises and clasps his hand warmly.

Johnny Oh, yes! This is the thing. I have missed this big
farmer's hand.

Cornelius There you are. That's why I always keep it by
me.

Johnny (*laughs*) Do you know, I think I'm listening to
the wrong radio station. I never hear anything but bad
news on mine. (*A moment.*) But, Cornelius, I have to say
it to you – by the hokey, man, I was at your funeral. Five
years ago.

Cornelius It was a day out for everyone.

Johnny Well, I don't know. Look, sit down there,
Cornelius, just in case. (*Locks the door.*) After all, when
you have someone else's organ sewn into your chest, for
the love of God. Whose heart do you have, Cornelius, by
the way?

Cornelius I never knew. I think it was the heart of a
young girl. I wrote a letter into the dark, and the
hospital gave it to the family of the donor.

Johnny I'm sure you performed that office well. You
always wrote a lovely letter.

Cornelius I'm of the mind that I always performed my offices well. When I was let.

Johnny Hmm. Hint of bitterness there.

Cornelius No, not bitterness. Truthfulness, Johnny.

Johnny In this country, Cornelius, the truth is the tripes of the animal. The thing the butcher cannot sell.

Cornelius It certainly did me little good.

Johnny True. (*pontificating*) There are areas of Belfast and Derry where the truth is the thing that will get you killed.

Cornelius That's the Northern way alright. But, sure, good luck to them.

Johnny The only people who survived Stalin's purges were the sick and the mad. What killed the others? The truth.

Cornelius Is that what killed the hunger-strikers, Johnny? The truth? I don't think so. Ah, well. Poor bastards.

Johnny Jesus, it was your woman killed the hunger-strikers. By Jesus, I tried to shift her. There isn't a dynamite invented could shift her. The fucking Baroness. I gave her hell over it. You know that.

Cornelius You gave her a teapot, a silver teapot.

Johnny Hey?

Cornelius Didn't you, though? As a memorial to your friendship. No?

> *Johnny says nothing. Cornelius wanders to the window, gazes out at the prospect.*

It is distant enough, this old house.

Johnny Hinterland of the city. Almost Dublin. The zoning is very advantageous. The fortunes I have thrown into it.

Cornelius It reminds me of the President's gaff.

Johnny Same damn architect. Genuine Georgeen, as they say down the markets. Two hundred thousand alone in the damned roof.

Cornelius I hoped once to be president myself.

Johnny Money, money, money, is the song an old house sings.

Cornelius I hoped once to be . . .

Johnny Well, yes, I know. And truly, Cornelius, the day I had to . . . knock that on the head as it were, was the day my interest in my own political advancement died. I thought I had to do it. I thought that by sacking you in a fair-handed manner, I might extend the life of the government, always a noble aim in a small country.

Cornelius (*dismissive, but a touch of emotion*) All water under the bridge now.

Johnny Such struggles, such days. And now. Lawyers, courts. Extraordinary things said to me! Could have been the death of a lesser man. In the spring it all starts again. Hanging over my head now like a bucket of shite. We just heard yesterday. Daisy, Daisy. Deeply, deeply wounding for her. Of course I have denied everything, every charge of impropriety, and years ago that would have sufficed. The word of an Irish gentleman of the old school. But in this dishonest era, everything you say is questioned. They won't play the game now. These fucking Supreme Court judges.

Cornelius I am sure they are good men enough.

Johnny Of course, of course. But little men. Does anyone know them? They live in great, concrete-cladded mausoleums out in the suburbs, with ridiculous gardens and knick-knacks from a hundred trips to Lourdes and Medugorja with their tired wives. Must I be judged by the likes of them?

Cornelius Ah well, fair dues to them.

Johnny Fellas without an ounce of poetry in them, unless it's Robert Service, some old fucker that their grandfathers used to read to them. e.e. cummings? I don't think so?

Cornelius Who?

Johnny And look, are they good men? We know nothing about them. They are beginning to know everything about us.

Cornelius They are better men than you or I. (*moving away*) You are talking to the wrong person, Johnny. After all, you killed me.

Johnny Journalists! Without journalists, I wouldn't have had to sack you. Dark-hearted drunken fellas with their grey, unhealthy bodies. That feel a lovely lessening of their own guilt, their own failure in their lives, when they hold up what they think is my history to the public gaze. I hear them on radio chat shows, you can almost smell the ooze of fake piety seep from them, disreputable raincoated characters that you'd shiver at, if your daughter brought one home. But for them I could have got you through, Cornelius. But for them!

Cornelius (*looking out*) Nice roses, though, in the summertime, I remember.

Johnny *Souvenir de St Anne's*. Cunts! The lot of them.

Cornelius Well, I think by tradition the Irish journalist has played an important role in history. Nationalism. The Irish press. The opposing view. De Valera and so on.

Johnny Would De Valera be proud of his country now? Every damn thing going to a tribunal. This account, that account – drink? – no? – the fucking Cayman Islands, who gives a fuck about all that, it was just money, not blood. (*Makes a drink for himself.*)

Cornelius Blood money. Judas in the Potter's Field.

Johnny Were we forever to live like slugs under the rock of the British economy? If we were careless in our financial dealings, weren't the fucking banks on our side? They are trying to hang us now – they are trying to hang me. It's ancient history!

Cornelius The trouble is, you prescribed the hair shirt for everyone else, even as you enriched yourself. I told you often enough to be mindful to die the day you stood down.

Johnny We were the judges of ourselves, and anyone who wasn't there in the thick of battle, with a twopenny-halfpenny country to turn into a modern state, has no right to go back through all that and say this and that was wrong. Other days, other ways. Let him who is without sin cast the first fucking stone.

Cornelius I don't know what to say to you. I have a vision of every Irish man and woman, with a bucket of stones at their sides, to throw at you. Oh, magnificent things you did. The pensioners sang your praises – St John of the Bus Pass. But by heavens, Johnny, you killed me.

Johnny (*a little desperate*) I made this country, whether they like it or not. They all voted for me when they thought it was to their advantage. How did those mealy-mouthed bastards and biddies get so high up they were heard and listened to? (*throwing himself into the chair*) It's like the Salem witch trials, the McCarthy era,

16

(*Cornelius goes quietly.*) the last years of Tsarist Russia, the Third Reich, Kristallnacht, is anyone safe? They will not give me my due now. I am to be ritually disembowelled in my own country, by my own countrymen. (*shouting*) That is my fate now! That is my fate now! (*as if waking*) Kiss me, Cornelius, kiss me!

He gets up dazedly, rubs his face, a knocking on the door.

Daisy (*off*) Johnny.

Johnny That can't be right. 'Cornelius, kiss me.'

Daisy (*off*) Johnny, Johnny, what is it? Open the door!

Johnny (*to himself, rubbing his face*) Is everything still true?

Daisy For God's sake, Johnny, what's going on?

He goes to the door, unlocks it.

Johnny I'm sorry, Daisy, I didn't know I'd locked it. Force of habit.

Daisy comes in, carrying a piece of Irish porcelain and a yellow cloth. She is a few years older than her husband, a solid woman who may once have been handsome. She has obviously been crying recently.

Daisy You've been roaring up the house. Jack leapt out of his bed in terror. He thought someone was trying to kill his father.

Johnny Where is he?

Daisy He went down to the kitchen to make himself a sandwich.

Johnny (*a sort of fatherly laugh*) Oh, ho. Well, I am fine, I am not wounded. Did the Special Branch man stir from his niche?

Daisy Not noticeably.

Johnny Will you have a nightcap with me, Daisy? (*Touches the teapot.*) Cold as the grave.

Daisy A nightcap? No.

Johnny Oh, have a drink with me, do, please. (*Pours another drink for himself.*)

Daisy No, thanks. Is there something amiss? This is not your routine.

Johnny Inform the papers! Nevertheless, nevertheless. Daisy, dear, are you –?

Daisy What?

Johnny (*at the table, looking into his teacup, smiling*) My Derry great-aunts could tell you the future from these tea leaves. The dregs. (*After a moment.*) I was asking if you were – alright?

Daisy Why wouldn't I be?

Johnny Exactly. Exactly.

Daisy I am always alright. It is my job. It was formerly, at any rate. I don't know about these days.

Johnny You don't?

Daisy I know less and less, these days. A woman like me should be going out to have her nice times. Hairdressers. Anti-aging facials. But how can I? All of Grafton Street, peering at me. There's your woman, the wife of you-know-who. Sometimes I think they will attack me, kill me, quench me like a candle.

Johnny Do they know your face, Daisy?

Daisy They know your face. And the sad face that sometimes floats beside it, or did, at functions, at excruciating functions. Less and less and less I know.

Johnny It will all be sorted out, in time. (*After a moment.*) Know less about me, and more about God. Mahatma Gandhi.

Daisy What does it mean?

Johnny I don't know! I always thought it was something he said to journalists. But maybe it wasn't. (*at the bottles*) What will you have, Daisy?

She doesn't answer.

Daisy?

Daisy (*staring at him a moment*) Nothing, Johnny. I don't want to drink anything. I didn't come in for that. I heard you shouting and was afraid, that's all. Or more afraid, I should say.

Johnny (*another drink*) What could you be afraid of, with the Special Branch man under the stairs, and Stephen prowling around worrying about the old catches on the windows?

Daisy I don't know. I wouldn't rest too much faith in that Special Branch man. I have a feeling he can sleep standing up like a horse.

Johnny He's a beatnik on his day off, apparently.

Daisy I was thinking about the old days, in my father's house. Suddenly I was there. And I felt better for those few moments. Of course, this porcelain was theirs. Flowers of Kew. And then there was this roaring, bringing me back.

Johnny And a very nice house he had indeed. They didn't begrudge him his achievements, political and financial.

Daisy Dad was the soul of probity, Johnny.

Johnny Probity? Is that the right word? Most decidedly he was.

Daisy I'll finish up with the porcelain and go to bed.

Johnny (*disappointed*) Well, alright. Chats, what happened to chats?

Daisy They ceased. Circa 1985.

Johnny Let's not go there, as the Yanks say.

Daisy Yes. I'm going down the country to see cousin Aggie tomorrow. I don't know what you're planning.

Johnny Oh, I'll linger here for the weekend. There's a student coming tomorrow. A PhD on the domestic history of Derry, whatever that is.

Daisy Hmm. Domestic, not your area of expertise. I think that's very unwise, if I may say so. At this time. To talk to anyone from the outside.

Johnny I think we're safe with the domestic history of Derry. My heavens, Daisy, it will be a relief to talk about something other than my bloody bank accounts. Stephen gave me the low-down. The very brightest of the bright at UCD, he says. At work on a very important chapter in the social history of the North. Probably be a book in the long term. 'It will be recreational for you,' he says, 'and an honour for her.' I'm looking forward to it.

Daisy It's a she then? Hmm. (*A moment, looking at him.*) Stephen could persuade a bull to dance a quickstep.

Johnny It will delight me to expatiate on these old matters. (*indicating the cupboard*) Anyway, I have a mountain of papers still to sort for the barristers. Now that the State Papers are gone, it leaves only accounts, letters, memos, a dreary set of records. The fruits of what some would call running the country with no time to attend to my own affairs.

Daisy I'm sure the country could have run itself. It always did in my father's time. He liked to tweak things just.

Johnny It takes more than tweaking in the modern world. And your father brought prosperity by borrowing great lumps of money, and putting the country into a long slough of debt, a slough I was still mopping up decades later. Of course, I admired him. I admire him still. I wish I had his history to call my own.

Daisy He had old-fashioned honesty.

Johnny Hmm.

Daisy Perhaps honesty is boring.

Johnny It's expensive anyway.

Daisy starting to go.

Daisy (*a moment*) You were in with a Dr Cunningham today, Stephen tells me. Why did you need to see him?

Johnny Stephen, the soul of discretion. (*A moment.*) What do you call it, palpitate the area.

Daisy Palpate, Johnny. What area would that be?

Johnny Hinterland.

Daisy Where?

Johnny Waterworks.

Daisy And? What did he say?

Johnny He said I was an old man, Daisy, that's the thing I remember him saying. (*After a moment.*) He said more than likely nothing. He took a . . . Going to ring me.

Daisy You ought to be able to speak to your wife in full sentences. Hinterland. Were you going to keep this a secret?

Johnny There's no secret, he's going to ring me. Was that a full sentence? Do you know, instead of grilling me, and looking at me like that, you might show a little – well, a modicum of tenderness? Solicitude? Not that I *require* a modicum of . . .

Daisy Being such a hard man of the old school.

They say nothing for a bit. He looks at her again and she's still staring.

Johnny What, what?

Daisy Nineteen eighty-five is the date that arises in my mind when the word 'secret' is uttered in this house. Secret, secret.

Johnny Oh, don't, now, come on. Nineteen eighty-five. Fifteen years ago.

Knock on door.

Daisy (*perhaps close to tears again*) I wonder why it seems like yesterday to me? Or tomorrow?

Johnny (*calling*) Who's that?

Daisy Rumours coming in under the front door like winter's rats. You were going on some official jaunt to Greece. And you turned in your polished shoes and said, 'Have you no sense of humour?'

Stephen It's Stephen, sir.

Daisy That's all you said.

Johnny It wasn't all I said. And what could I say? It didn't seem – real. Come in, Stephen. (*to Daisy, quickly*) Connie, it didn't seem to connect, another life, another planet – absurd. It embarrassed me.

Stephen comes in.

Daisy Embarrassed you?

Johnny Well. Stephen? I thought you were gone to your rest.

Stephen Do you have everything you want?

Johnny Allow me to reflect on that. Yes, I think so.

Stephen I've turned down your bed, Mrs Silvester.

Daisy Oh, thanks, Stephen.

Stephen And put in the hot-water bottle. (*Fetches tea tray.*)

Daisy Ceramic.

Stephen Ceramic.

Johnny Ceramic?

Daisy It is a consolation of sleeping alone, you can have a ceramic hot-water bottle if you wish, that reminds you of your childhood.

Stephen Goodnight, then. (*He goes.*)

Johnny Goodnight, Stephen.

Daisy (*taking up again where she left off*) Out the door with you and into the state car and up the road to the airport. I was left here all week, and I thought I would go mad.

Johnny That's not true. I phoned you. Sent you flowers.

Stephen again.

Stephen Cocoa?

Johnny No.

Stephen Yourself, Mrs Silvester?

Johnny No.

Daisy Me neither. Thank you.

Stephen Very good. (*Goes.*)

Daisy A woman like that, a feckless, foolish, self-regarding . . . I sat in this house crying, like some devil was throwing poison over the part of me that feels pleasure. The whole house was pouring with smoke, I thought. But it was just the smoke of my life, all the weird little things you have said over the years. I was born a politician's daughter and I know the life. I know the triumph of men like you, when the whole world votes for you and you are made King of Ireland.

Johnny Is that so bad?

Daisy I know what that does to the little families of such men. Jack and me, when Jack was small. A little boy, waiting for his father to come home. (*After a little.*) Do you know what a little boy is, Johnny? I'll tell you. He's a tiny contraption of bones and skin, tuned like a radio to give out and receive certain signals. When a little boy is sick, his whole body strains to broadcast a special signal, he wants a very simple thing, to be cuddled there in the arms of his father. Does that sound sentimental to you?

Johnny No. It sounds ominous.

Daisy And not just times of sickness. Ordinary days, ordinary hours. The simple moments of childhood. The little boy sets up his coloured blocks and waits for his father to come and arrange them with him. He waits and waits. It would need, heavens, only a minute of play to assuage that strange hunger, Johnny. Maybe you remember it yourself, when you were little?

Johnny My old man had multiple sclerosis, Daisy. You bloody well know that, Daisy. (*angrily, trying to suppress* *it*) You can hardly expect a shadow in a bed to attend to his fatherly duties! A shadow-man!

Daisy Poor you, yes, poor you, poor Johnny. I pity all the little boys of this world. Because, when the signal is not answered, the pain is so great, so oddly great. I've seen it, I've looked at it. If the father does not come, does not ever come, the little boy finally kicks at the blocks and breaks them asunder, he wants to turn them into dust.

Johnny Don't, Daisy, you'll break my heart.

Daisy And the pity is, no one can stack those few blocks again, no one can put the boy back on the floor, sitting there waiting, no one can do anything about it, it becomes sort of lost in time. (*A moment.*) A true father would feel that call from three thousand miles and travel all day and night to reach his child. Nothing can put that little scenario back together again and time goes on swiftly and then there is nothing but a tangle of broken wires, good for nothing because it can finally neither receive nor send a signal. Do you understand me?

Johnny Only the greatest fool on earth would not understand you, Daisy.

Daisy You were running for office, or running the country. Ah, yes. But it denies something at the heart of life. At the heart of families, of countries, of political parties even. If that slight signal is not attended to, there really is no family, party or country. Because the oldest law on earth has been violated.

Johnny You're a very wise woman, Daisy Silvester. But I hope you're not going to say all that to me and then go to bed and leave me here, to think about it?

Daisy Why not?

Johnny Why not, indeed?

Daisy (*getting up*) Nineteen eighty-five. When I think on it.

Johnny Daisy, give over, do. I'm an old man now. It's official!

Daisy Then I must be an old woman. Defunct. Do you know, it isn't so much that dreadful woman, but all those dinners, journeys, hotel holidays you had with her – the mere cost of it. The steaks, the lobsters, the champagne. By God. When I think of it. And I do think of it. That book of hers – I didn't want to read it – I picked it up in the supermarket. What am I trying to say? I don't know.

Johnny Poor . . .

Daisy Don't poor Daisy me! (*A moment.*) She took all my holidays from me.

Johnny It wasn't holidays. I was working. Running a certain little country? Is cousin Aggie expecting you, Daisy?

Daisy Why?

Johnny Just, to make an arrangement like that, without –

Daisy Clearance?

Johnny Oh, no.

Daisy Oh, yes. I am still just a minor ministry in your government. The department of the blessed wife. It was given to you to stand on the world stage and be counted among the leaders of Europe, and to go hither and thither. Like Dad. But all Mammy expected of Dad was the dignity of his love, the signs of his faithfulness, and his gracious way of talking to her. You watched him so carefully, and copied him in many things. Except that.

Johnny Ah, look it. How many times do you need to bring this up?

Daisy (*enraged*) I'll bring it up as many times as I need to, till I feel better about it! This is a conversation about your infidelity to me, Johnny. Putting yourself about. Glad rags.

Johnny Is it? Yes, yes, of course it is. Yes, but. Have you no sense of humour, girl? I mean.

Daisy You see? You see? You did say that.

Johnny (*smiling, lightly*) You're just pissed off with me, in a general way.

Daisy I want a life in the present. Everything about me is years ago. I want to live and breathe in present times. Think in the present, love in the present.

Johnny And you do, and you will.

Daisy I get so sick of being a passenger on your leaky old boat.

Johnny You know I've cut all contact with Connie. You said yourself, we could both look forward to a more dignified future. You kissed me. Three months ago, that's all it was. It took you fifteen years to forgive me!

Daisy No, it took you fifteen years to give her up! I know what the Irish people think of me. Dull little Daisy Silvester. The contempt other women must have for me.

Johnny Well, look, we sorted it out, we sorted out our own affairs, in private, amicably, lovingly. Try and think of it that way, Daisy. Is it Jack has you done down?

Daisy That would be very convenient. He has enough to put up with without providing excuses for you.

Johnny (*smiling*) You don't like me any more, Daisy. Is that what it is? Beatniks are flourishing but love is extinct!

Daisy Yes. Maybe that's it, right enough. (*again almost to herself, turning half away*) It is all such a sorry . . . I am too exhausted for this, too . . . Disasters come in threes, they say. First that terrible book of hers, then the resumption date of your trial. What next? (*suddenly, without exhaustion*) That bloody woman. Why did she do that to me? If I had her at my mercy I would crush her underfoot. As something that crawls on the earth.

A timid knock on the door.

Johnny Hmm?

Daisy (*dragging back his attention*) If you ever speak to her again, if you ever . . . I will fetch out my mother's old carving knife!

Johnny To do what, Daisy?

Jack (*outside*) Can I come in, Daddy?

She is trembling. Johnny stares at her as if she was a wild beast suddenly in the room. He sits down on his chair, staring, licking his dry lips.

Johnny Come in, come in, Jack. Why not?

Jack, his son, thirty years old, comes in dutifully carrying a sandwich on a blue-and-white plate. He wears a Walkman headpiece around his neck and carries the cassette player in one hand.

Hiya, Jack. Where did you find that old plate for your sandwich?

Jack It's the only old plate in the kitchen.

Johnny It's from the farmhouse in Derry. A memento. A keepsake.

Jack I like it.

Johnny Good for you. Historical. I'm sorry I gave you a fright earlier.

Jack Earlier?

Johnny Your mother said you heard me roaring.

Jack Oh, yes. I – I was reminded of poor bulls, you know, when you have to – turn them into bullocks, I suppose.

Johnny (*looking at Daisy*) Well! You are speaking as a vet, of course.

Jack (*shakily*) I am speaking as a vet – as an ex-vet. Do you want half of this? (*proffering the sandwich*) Corned beef.

Johnny I will, I will. I was taught never to decline food. The Derry farm was run with the black face of poverty pressed to the window outside. I've been bloody careful therefore to gather a sufficiency for us all, and a little something over. You can't have enough money, Jack. Remember that when I am . . .

Daisy When you are what?

> *Johnny looks at her, decides not to answer. Jack puts the Walkman down in the State Papers cupboard to give his father the sandwich.*

Johnny The famous Walkman. What were you listening to?

Jack Verdi. Moby.

Johnny Verdi's *Moby Dick*? Did he write about the Great White Whale? Do you remember, Daisy, they made that in Ireland – John Huston. When they were bringing Moby Dick on a lorry over Chapelizod Bridge, it overturned and crushed a man in a bubble car. It was in the papers! And they moored Moby Dick at Howth, and one dark night in a storm the fish broke free, and went sailing out into the Irish Sea, and was never seen again.

Daisy Chats.

Johnny (*to Jack*) Captain Ahab, Gregory Peck, et cetera?

Jack No, Daddy. Moby – the singer. (*Half-sings.*)
   Oh Lordy, trouble so hard,
   Oh Lordy, trouble so hard . . .

   Johnny shrugging.

Johnny A more useful song than any of Verdi's, at the moment. (*examining sandwich*) Where's the beef?

Daisy For once in your life you get the poor half of the sandwich!

   Jack gives his father some of the beef out of his half of the sandwich.

Johnny On that note, Jack. (*eating*) I know you've been through a hard time recently. But . . . These lawyers and journalists. Watch your back. Father, son. Sometimes they like to make no distinction. Tar with the same brush.

   Jack looks at Daisy in alarm.

Jack What brush, Mammy?

Daisy Oh, Johnny.

Johnny No, no, it has implications for him. Once they have you where they want you, they'll continue to press their heel down hard. Even I've been astonished by the ferocity and tenacity of their attack. But I don't fear them. They'll tie me down, and open my stomach, and feed my guts to the pigs, like the lads did to each other in the civil war, but I won't cry out. However.

Jack I've never heard you talk like this, Daddy. I had no idea they might be interested in me. What have I done?

Johnny Nothing, nothing. But so what? What have I done? No. It becomes a fashion, a fashion of justice. (*quickly, mostly to Jack*) Even your mother is against me now.

Daisy Oh, please.

Johnny The fashion for justice against old Johnny Silvester has got a grip on her too. (*Daisy oddly starts to cry.*)

Jack I am. I am . . . going to eat this sandwich.

Johnny (*to Jack*) I'm sorry, Jack. A father should never seek the sympathy of his son. It is obscene and absurd.

Jack stares at them both.

Jack No matter what they say, Daddy, I'm on your side. I will defend you. (*Holds up the sandwich.*)

Johnny You will defend me with a sandwich? Very good. But thank you, Jack, thank you. (*to Daisy*) Are you crying? Why are you crying?

Jack looks at his mother. Now he is suddenly quietly crying, the plate at an angle. Johnny comes over, levels the plate.

Your father is very gloomy tonight. Forgive me. I was always an optimist.

Jack I have a pain in my head, Daddy. Frightened.

Johnny Go on with yourself. Doctors. Charlatans. Depression. My backside. The finest veterinarian student of your year, Jack! You must get back to your horses and cows. That will restore you.

Jack (*at the pictures, simply, suddenly relaxed*) You really should keep water-colours out of direct sunlight. These old pictures are fading. You can't restore water-colours.

Johnny I used to take great joy from this room. All these signs and tokens of my standing in the world. Vanity, vanity, all is vanity. The smaller I get, the better fit will

I be to enter heaven, unless heaven too is to be debarred me. I wonder how God feels about Irish politics? What do you think? I've gone from king to criminal in the space of a couple of years. Did I not serve this country well? Did I not create this plenty they enjoy now? I couldn't have done what I have done without being the man I was and the man I am. Nor could I have done it without the complicity of a hundred other like-minded men. There was no other way. They needed a clear-minded man, who understood what the real world was. And I gave them their paradise of European roads, and low unemployment. They are on the pig's back. The only thing lacking now is the killing of the golden goose, the slaughtering of the scapegoat. But I am no Ceauscescu, I am no Stalin, no Hitler, no sullen killer in the Balkans. There is not a drop of blood on these hands, Jack. But they should be careful what stones they shift. Many a queer fact, many a queer insect will come scuttling out. Ah, Jack, forgive me, I'm away again. And I was trying to put your mind at ease! You look like you've just seen a ghost.

Jack Do I? Have I?

Johnny What a fine little boy you were. Intelligent, intelligent. You want to get back to your cows, Jack. (*He holds Jack's face in his hands a moment, moves on.*)

Jack (*stranded, more to himself*) I couldn't. I couldn't go back, at the moment.

Johnny Hah?

Jack (*quietly, lucidly*) I do miss everything. Yes. Talking to the farmers, joking, knowing what to do. My life.

Daisy Jack.

> *They say nothing for a while. Jack seems to give up, goes to door.*

Johnny (*suddenly*) You'll get back to it, for God's sake, you'll get back to it.

Daisy Of course he will.

Jack You know I love you, Daddy. From the age of five I rarely saw you.

Johnny glances at Daisy.

When you got going in the politics. I suppose I should resent it. But there is something about you, Daddy. I like you, is what it is. Goodnight, Daddy. Goodnight, Mam.

Johnny (*astounded*) Goodnight, goodnight.

They stand there a moment. Jack goes.
Johnny sits in his chair, clasping his jacket about himself, shivering. He looks at Daisy. She's in a daze. Shakes his head.

Johnny Jesus, it's getting cold in here. What the hell is going on? I trust you didn't turn off the heating.

He gets up and goes to the radiator under the window.

It's still going strong. Maybe the temperature has dropped outside. (*Kicks the radiator.*) These fucking old houses. You can't keep them warm. And this is a little room. It must be arctic in the drawing room? My father's house was always like a tomb. But he hadn't the shekels.

He walks up and down, swinging his arms into his sides like a countryman.

This is how we did it in the old days. What say you, Daisy?

Daisy (*after a moment*) These are the old days, Johnny.

Johnny Hey? (*After a moment.*) Well, Daisy, Daisy – what will we do with the boy?

Daisy Do? You don't do anything – I mean, one doesn't do anything. As long as he takes the medication.

Johnny So they have him on the tablets still?

Daisy You know this, Johnny. And if you don't know it . . .

Johnny Yes, yes, but . . . Fatherly concern, detailed questions, plans. Because you have brought him through, Daisy. I understand that. The nightmares, the walking about the house, that's all ceased. And the gabbling, thinking he was going to be arrested. For what?

Daisy Taking your plight on himself. Delusion. As long as he takes the medication . . . That was the struggle. Two years.

Johnny John of Gods. That gloomy building, those long, drugged faces. Young people . . . Our own country! But from where, from what? There were no madmen in my family.

Daisy's face.

Daisy You always said your mother's family lot were a crowd of lunatics, Johnny. I was never sure your mother wasn't a sandwich short of a picnic herself.

Johnny My mother had a hard time of it. Eccentric, I accept that. Nursing her own husband, day in, day out. The bleak, dark mountain of MS. Ravaged. Worn away. A piece of bog oak, and then, at length, a twig. So what now? What hope for Jack? Can he go back to his work?

Daisy (*after a moment, softening*) Take it a day at a time. Like any other mortal tragedy. Accept the situation. Say, this is how it is.

Johnny What's going to happen to him?

Daisy (*gently, coming near him*) Don't worry, Johnny. God will help us. (*She touches his face briefly.*)

Johnny (*he doesn't dare move*) Him? Well. Maybe. You've borne the brunt of it. I'm well aware. Poor Daisy. Poor Jack.

Daisy Poor Johnny. (*Suddenly, she slaps his face hard with her hand.*)

Johnny Holy God, girl, why did you do that?

Daisy It came into my mind to do it. And I did it. That bloody woman. A moment of tenderness, and she always intrudes into my mind.

Johnny Look, that bloody woman is out of the picture. Do you hear? I will never, never, never, never, never – *Samson Agonistes*, the perfect reversed iambic pentameter, do you understand? Never!

Daisy Is that Samson Agonistes talking or Johnny Silvester?

Johnny Johnny Agonistes.

Daisy (*at the door*) I'll go up. I hope I didn't hurt you. I hope I hurt you. You killed me.

Johnny Hah, Daisy? That's exactly what Cornelius said.

Daisy Cornelius? Prescient man.

Johnny You don't think that, do you, Daisy?

Daisy Everyone thinks that, Johnny. You're a gobshite, Johnny, really. You know nothing about yourself. You're like a little child. A very dangerous little child with the strength of a man.

Johnny But I don't understand, how did I . . .?

Daisy (*laughing a little*) Goodnight, Johnny.

Johnny Goodnight, goodnight, Daisy.

She goes. He walks quietly to the open door, listening to her footsteps going upstairs. He goes back to the desk and turns on the radio. Classical music plays.

Too late in the day for the poise and clarity of the eighteenth century. (*He roughly turns off the radio.*) Alone. (*After a moment.*) Am I? (*His face is drawn and ashen now. Counting again, one, two, three. Holds the breath, releases it.*) Stress management. Guilt management. Oh creeping intimations of hideous lapses . . . Oh fuck, oh fuck, oh fuck, oh fuck, oh fuck.

Suddenly Cornelius is behind him.

Cornelius You could sing that if you had a tune for it.

Johnny Brendan Behan, hah? (*without looking at him*) I'm mighty tired, Cornelius. I wonder, do you have the secret of a good night's sleep?

Cornelius A clear conscience, so they say. Conventional wisdom.

Johnny Conventional wisdom won't cut the mustard, Cornelius. The Spanish say, the best aspirin is death. Or so Hemingway would have you believe. *For Whom the Bell Tolls.* A clear conscience. I have never heretofore suffered much from guilt, conscience and the like. I know people think that's curious. But I think I famished myself with guilt years ago. My sister.

Cornelius But, Johnny, you don't have a sister, do you?

Johnny I was only small myself. I had a journalist say to me once, I can't imagine you as a child, Mr Silvester. But I was, I was – like everybody else. She was about a year old, just walking, the baby. Beatrice. I was so excited by her coming, damn me. I couldn't get enough of her. Well, that winter I contracted scarlet fever, and my aunts came

36

down from Derry to help. I was old enough to have it without much harm. I was soon out of bed. Quarantine, two weeks. They told me, 'Don't go in to Beatrice, Johnny,' Aunt Winnie held me by the shoulders and drummed it into me. I was just a little boy, and full of beans, and full of love. One afternoon, I crept in to Beatrice, napping in her cot, when no one was watching, and gave her a hug and crept away again. It was just love, Cornelius, this saving grace of love.

Cornelius Oh, dear.

Johnny It was a mystery to them. There was heartbreak. They didn't know how it had happened. I said I didn't know. It became a kind of dark history. Sometimes at night I still wake up. I wish I had confessed to it. Awful stuff at your back, you know?

Cornelius Poor Johnny now.

Johnny (*matter-of-factly*) It was my fault.

Cornelius What age were you?

Johnny Four and a half.

Cornelius You weren't to blame, are you crazy, Johnny?

Johnny Nevertheless. She died. Today is her anniversary, oddly enough.

Cornelius You can put all thought of blame from your mind, Johnny. That is what is called a tragedy.

Johnny (*a moment.*) Never explain, never say you're sorry. Who said that?

Cornelius Zeb McCain, *How the West was Won.*

Johnny I'm impressed, Cornelius.

Cornelius Some things I know.

Johnny Although that has been my general rule, I want to state that I was aware of the ramifications of what I did to you, its implications. I knew you were recovering from that lousy operation, and yet . . .

Cornelius It was the drugs they were giving me, put me in a muddle. Lapse of memory.

Johnny But you contradicted yourself in public on a very sensitive issue at a time when contradiction was potentially ruinous. There we were, assailed by every imaginable thing, beef barons and their toxic meat, and everything starting to be laid at my door, and things generally going to hell. It was not a moment to falter, Cornelius. (*After a moment.*) All I want to say is, I was aware. But survival, that is the first principle. The party.

Cornelius On the first day, you announced that my candidature for president was unassailable. Oh, I sang your praises in my bed that night, grateful. On the second day, you cut off my head.

Johnny I can't apologise, even for such a grievous thing. It would be inappropriate. But I can say, I was aware.

Cornelius You behaved so cruelly, Johnny, unsurpassed cruelty. I went up to the Iveagh Gardens and walked there among the ruined avenues for an hour. I was shaken. I was deathly shaken. I don't know if a man could ever imagine such distress, unless he has been through it. I was hanging on to life, and I needed that election, because it would guarantee something, time, a future. I could imagine being that elected person. I had a vision of it. And when everything was taken away, suddenly, in all that confusion, by my closest friend, a man I had defended and loved through everything, I became another person – another Cornelius, walking in the Iveagh Gardens, with a heavy heart.

Johnny I'm sorry, Cornelius. I'm sorry.

Cornelius Well, well . . .

Johnny (*a moment*) And what good did it do? None. You fucked up, I fucked up. Then Ireland had a bloody woman president, with her selfless bloody tone, and we were off willy-nilly on our little voyage to the scrap-heap.

Cornelius It's all cold soup now. God knows.

Johnny God knows. All my beautiful secrets, uncovering one by one, ticking like bombs. And you dying on me. And I had striven to raise the cash to try and save you. Did you know that?

Cornelius You did mention it.

Johnny I would not like to tell you what they accuse me of, these bleak times, *vis-à-vis* that very money. No filthy greed, no miserable skullduggery, is beyond their imaginations, when it comes to me. If I could turn back the clock, Cornelius . . .

Cornelius You would do the same thing. And what do they accuse you of, *vis-à-vis* the money?

Johnny What else, but that I spent it on myself.

Cornelius And did you, Johnny?

Johnny On my life, Cornelius . . .

Cornelius It doesn't matter anyhow.

Johnny It does matter. What do you mean, it doesn't fucking matter?

Cornelius You don't understand, do you, Johnny? The fires are being stoked for you in another place. And I don't mean the British House of Lords.

Johnny Then our childhood fears – all true?

Cornelius All true, heaven, hell, angels, God, the lot.

Johnny How can I escape? Act of contrition? You've helped me out of sticky situations before.

Cornelius I am fearful for you. While I have crossed the bar myself, I don't know rightly what will become of you. The fires meanwhile are certainly being stoked. Oh, yes.

He goes away back through the cupboard.

Johnny (*trying to follow him, speaking into the cupboard*) Listen here, Cornelius, there must be something? Some gesture? Of piety, of love? Cornelius? (*alone*) This is fear. I'm frightened. Picture of childhood. The flames. Johnny, what are you? Madness? Enter Lear dressed fantastically in wild flowers. (*attempting a prayer*) *Confiteor deo omnipotenti – beato Ioanni Baptistae – mea culpa, mea culpa* . . . Cornelius?

Half-singing, pacing:

I wish the Queen of England would send for me in
    time,
And place me in some regiment all in my youth and
    prime,
And I'd fight for Ireland's glory from the clear daylight
    of the dawn,
And I never would return again for to plough the
    Rocks of Bawn . . .

A moment.

Fuck ya, Cornelius!

He clicks off the light and goes out, and heads up the stairs himself. His footsteps dying away.
At length, a knock on the door.

Daisy Johnny, Johnny. Are you there?

She comes in, sits in the darkness on his chair.
Eventually takes up phone and dials.

Hello, Aggie? It's me. It's dreadfully late – I'm sorry. Just want to confirm we're coming down tomorrow. (*listening*) Johnny won't be coming. (*listening*) Sometimes I think, that's it, this man is definitely going senile. Next moment, sharp as an axe. (*listening*) The tribunal again in the spring. When we should be looking forward to the daffodils coming up in the gardens! He sits here in this room of his, most of the time, pretending to be working. (*listening*) He's not facing up to things, taking on board what's happening to him. The essence of it is, we're old people. Retired. As if. It all seems very cruel. (*listening*) Alright, Aggie, dear. Tomorrow. Yes. I'll see you then.

Stephen appears in the door, in his pyjamas and
dressing gown, nice slippers. He is probably making
sure she is alright.

You gave me a fright, Stephen. Are you not gone down to bed long ago?

Stephen Yes, I am tired enough. But I was worrying.

A moment. She questions him with a look.

The window-latch. (*He checks it.*)

Daisy Oh.

Stephen Hmmm.

Daisy Well, there.

Stephen says nothing.

Will you go to Torremolinos again this year?

Stephen (*after a moment*) Nerja. (*A moment.*) My sister has the holiday flat in Nerja.

Daisy That's right.

A moment. Stephen going again. Daisy bestirs herself.

I'll go too.

> *They go out together, her hand lightly on his back,
> leaving the door open.*

*

*The room in darkness, alone, something of a character
itself, the strange small-hour tick of time, the moon
rising, the stars freshening, the light shifting on the
mementos, the awards, the citations, at the pace of sleep,
of a person a-dream.*

*Now it is the small hours of the night, a spare clean
darkness in the windows, a lost wind outside gusting.*

*A figure comes in, wearing a dressing gown, but
indistinct. The person stands in the room, then climbs
on to the desk, and seems to examine the cord of the
light above. He removes the cord of his dressing gown,
and starts to tie the two together.*

Act Two

As before, the figure tugs on the light cord to test it, but it pulls away, and a lump of plaster comes clattering down. He pulls again, and the cord drags from the centre of the room to the point above the switch, sending more plaster falling. He stands there with the cord in his hand, flummoxed.

Johnny (*off*) Special Branch! Special Branch! Merciful God, I'll see to it myself.

Johnny comes in the door wielding a poker and turns on the light. The bulb comes alive in the figure's hand. It's Jack. The surprise of it sets him tottering. Johnny rushes forward and steadies him by holding his lower legs.

Christ, Jack. What are you doing, old fellow? (*desperately*) This is no time of the night to be checking the wiring. It was McCormack wired this house in the seventies. But it was a nixer, you know?

Jack There's no come-back on a nixer.

Johnny Exactly. (*After a moment.*) Was it what I said to you earlier? I only said those things to prepare you, to make you strong. I'm sorry if I upset you.

Jack You didn't upset me. I was feeling – bleak, is all it was.

He starts to climb down, Johnny assisting, but he trips and falls to the floor. Johnny kneels to him.
He cries.

43

Jack I'm sorry, I'm sorry.

Johnny Hey, hey, desist. All manner of things will be well. 'The woods decay, the woods decay and fall. Man comes to till the field and lies beneath, and after many a summer dies the swan.' After many a summer, Jack. You remember your Tennyson, eh? That's all it is.

Jack After many a summer. Can't bear it, Daddy.

Johnny (*humorously*) Things fall apart, the ceiling cannot hold.

Daisy (*from the open door*) What are you saying to him? (*coming in*) What's all this – the ceiling? Jack?

Jack's pleading face to Johnny.

Johnny (*a moment*) He was helping me.

Daisy What were you doing down, Jack?

Johnny He was – wandering.

Daisy Come on, Jack, let's go back up.

Johnny It's alright, Daisy, I'm dealing with it.

Daisy Listen, you can be the king that ruined his country, but I won't let you be the father that ruined his son.

Johnny I'm doing my best. What you said. Coloured blocks. Signals. The boy is upset, can't you see?

Daisy I'll bring him back to bed. (*to Jack*) Do up your dressing gown. Where's the cord?

Jack indicates where it is, unties it from the light cord.

Daisy Oh, my God.

Johnny I want to talk to him. Straighten matter out.

Daisy You can't.

She helps Jack up.

Jack I'd rather stay here with Daddy.

Daisy Sitting on the floor in a rain of plaster? You can take your sleeping pill. Everything measured and peaceful. That's what you need.

Johnny Measured and peaceful. That would be most welcome.

Daisy Don't be sarcastic with me, you bastard.

Johnny Bastard, now? Where does bastard come from? Words leaping at me! How come, bastard? I have been following your intimations and instructions assiduously.

Daisy You are being asinine. I was speaking of things years ago. When the chance was there for being a good father. Long, long, long ago.

Jack I think he is a good father, Mam.

Johnny What is it, Daisy? Last time we met, three thousand years ago, around midnight, it was gentleness, understanding, hand on face –

Daisy Gentleness? I struck you!

Johnny – now it's the old hag act again, cursing at me. Like some decrepit Cassandra, some vengeful Aisling. Hey? What is it bothers you now? About this? Is it that I love my son? And that he loves me? I adore him. He adores me. It bothers you? You wish to erase it?

Daisy I wish to go back to bed.

Jack Who's Aisling?

Johnny (*ignoring him*) You see, I'm lying up there in my bed alone, and I'm thinking, what's all this about blocks and fathers and – did I do this to Jack? Is that what you meant? Are you sure it wasn't yourself, Daisy? When he was eleven, he wouldn't take off his anorak in the house. You indulged it. He wouldn't let anyone cut his hair. You indulged it. Molly-coddling, molly-coddling. It would soften anyone's head!

Jack But, Daddy, I'm fine now, I'm fine, I'm getting better.

They say nothing for a little.

Johnny Of course you are. Excuse me.

Jack Who's Aisling?

Daisy (*ignoring him*) Talking about him, in front of him, as if he didn't exist. The bare savagery of it. And blaming me. My God, a person regrets any kindness shown to you. (*differently, with the previous softness*) So this is official, is it? You accuse me?

Johnny I don't, I don't. (*A moment.*) An Aisling, Jack, is Ireland personified by a young woman, in many a plaintive Irish poem of the eighteenth century, when the number was up with the old order of chieftains and kings. Jesus! What's the point? (*Head down, a moment, the energy deserting him.*) I know the name of this river, methinks, Johnny Silvester. It is the lovely waterway they call Shit Creek.

The phone ringing.

Johnny Four in the morning. Hardly Dr Mengele. If that's that fucking journalist . . . (*He lifts the receiver.*) Who's that? (*surprised*) Sean Day? Jesus, you know what time . . . Yeh, I see. Well, there's no truth in it. (*Daisy starting to go with Jack*) Hold on a sec. (*hand over receiver*) Daisy, Daisy. (*to Sean*) No. News travels fast. Yeh, it would be understandable, I suppose. Stress, Sean. Do you know what time it is? Los Angeles? That's eight hours difference. If I'd known what your counting was like, I'd never have made you Minister of Finance. What? Only joking. That's good of you. I appreciate it.

A few flakes fall from the ceiling.

I'll have to say goodnight. I'm dealing with a small problem here. The ceiling is coming down. No, not metaphorically. Really. Goodnight, Sean. Many thanks. Yeh.

Puts down receiver. When he turns around, Daisy and Jack are gone.

Daisy! (*to himself*) I wanted to suggest something . . . A plan, a plan is the thing. A programme for good self-government. (*After a moment, he lowers his head and sets it on the cold phone.*) Somebody's thinking about me, even if it's only that fool Sean Day.

Johnny stands there. Passing of time, morning, the weak early sunlight sneaks in from the gardens. Then fuller sunlight, cloudburst, rain. Stephen enters slowly. He surveys the mess of plaster.

Stephen What happened here, Mr Silvester?

Johnny Would you ever be so kind as to fetch me a cup of Earl Grey?

Stephen I will, certainly. There's a television crew setting up in the outer hall, Mr Silvester.

Johnny Hah??

Stephen Not politics! A little programme about the Blasket Islands. I said you would probably talk to them, briefly. And there is a girl to see you, as arranged, a very pretty girl from the university.

Johnny I can't see anyone till I wash and change. If you see Mrs Silvester on your travels about the place, will you ask her to pop her head in later? I'll talk to the TV crowd first. You could show the young woman in here. Maybe run the broom over it. (*on his way out*) Oh, there you are, Daisy.

Daisy (*off*) Here I am.

Johnny I was looking for you. How's the boy?

Daisy I managed to – I have these horse-pills his doctor gave me.

Johnny (*a moment*) I have an idea. Why don't we go next week to France, just you and me, and have a dekko at some of those gardens you like, you know, those big places, statues and so on, avenues, vistas, Le Notre, the works?

Daisy Why?

Johnny What do you mean?

Daisy Why? What's the point?

Johnny Oh, yes, I get you now. The point. The point would be, to say sorry for last night. I mean, not just last night. What you were saying, about going out, you know, for facials. You know what I mean. I think it might be nice. And before all the legal shenanigans start again. It might help me too, settle the mind for the fray. You and me, Daisy. Eh?

Daisy You and me, Johnny? What about Jack?

Johnny Well, maybe cousin Aggie . . . No? – maybe we could bring him, like the old days.

Daisy What mythical old days are those?

Johnny Well, just think about it, Daisy. Next week. When you come back from Aggie's? My heavens, is France not the very home of anti-aging creams?

Daisy glances at Stephen, goes out again. Stephen's face blank with listening.

Well! To work! To the boudoir!

Stephen If you want to avoid the crew, you could go up by the old servants' stairs, Mr Silvester. It's a bit of a squeeze.

Johnny (*going out*) Was there never such a thing as a fat servant?

Stephen Not in my experience. It's the diet.

Stephen fetches a broom and dustpan, starts to sweep up plaster. Sunlight waxes and wanes and alters the colours of things.

Wrecking the place, and then it's the likes of me has to clean up. These bloody people, treating you like – (*the plaster*) dirt. Cup of tea. Ever so kind. (*Pauses with the broom.*) At this hour of day my father God rest him would've been tending to the heifers in the haggard. That's noble work. Whereas I . . . (*He stops at the window, looks out.*) Look at him, going about like he was something important. Why isn't he in here guarding Mr Silvester? Hey! (*Puts down the dustpan and opens the window.*) Would you ever keep off the rose-beds, Mr Special Branch Man!

Special Branch Man (*off, distantly, discreetly*) Fuck off!

Stephen (*retrieving himself, shutting the window*) Oh!

He goes out with the full dustpan. After a little he returns with a woman of about nineteen, bright-faced, thick rope of hair.

Here you are. The inner sanctum. The lair of the lion.

Aisling Oh. I am nervous. My stomach is all over the place.

Stephen Lion, maybe not. And if he is a lion, the old lion is a bit low these times.

Aisling I'm sorry to hear it. Do you know, I didn't think you would grant me the interview.

Stephen Ask him nice, easy questions, why don't you.

Aisling (*pleasantly*) It's just a few questions about Derry, in the thirties, when his father was young. Oh my God, I was up all night trying to think of good ones. I even rang my father – but he wasn't much help.

Stephen Go easy on him, anyway. He's not well, you see. Hush-hush. Mustn't talk about it. Special Branch man, no discretion whatsoever. Mr Silvester was at the clinic yesterday. Waiting for a phone call now. Yes, yes. Waterworks, you know.

Aisling Poor man.

Stephen Oh, well, well, an old tom cat. Bears his scars. (*humorously*) Sit well back – I always tell the young ladies that. I'll bring you some tea in a minute. I'm never far away.

Aisling Thanks very much.

Stephen There he is now. He'll be talking to the television first. (*Goes.*)

She takes her notebook and tape recorder from her cloth bag and stands there holding everything. She listens as Johnny's voice is heard distantly, talking to the TV crew.

Johnny (*off*) Modest lives . . . lived frugally . . . amid great beauty. The Blaskets, another country, country of the heart . . . of dreams.

Aisling Mother of God . . .

His steps approach. Now Johnny enters dressed to the nines, grave, statesmanlike. The TV lights, shining in from the far hall, make a vision of him for a moment.

(*He takes her hand solemnly.*) How do you do? I'm Johnny Silvester. (*indicating the lights*) The Blaskets. The islands. I love the islands.

Aisling It's very nice to meet you, Mr Silvester.

Johnny Derry? Ah, me. So many years ago.

Aisling Aisling Dwyer. I'm from Dublin actually. Derry is my subject at the moment. Have to write about something – choose something. So why not, I said – fashionable, poignant, important, you know?

Johnny Aisling. A very nice Irish name. Please, sit down, be at your ease.

Aisling Thank you. Of course, I take the subject seriously. And I am anxious to learn more. My suspicion is, the condition of Derry before the Troubles was the ground on which the Troubles were erected. So by investigating, I am hoping to find illumination – but, actually, I want to be an actress.

She sits, he sits himself. He smiles.

Johnny (*resignedly*) So, fire away, Aisling.

Aisling Of course, I know acting is a hard profession. (*getting out her notes*) I used to think, if they have a script, sure, don't they know what's coming next? And therefore, isn't it a simple matter? But, of course, when you know what's coming next, nothing is simple, because you're anticipating, and that's a great sin for an actor, I'm told. Of course, I could go and read to be a lawyer, I've got the grades for that anyway. My father says, never change horses in mid-stream. He's a Bob

Dylan fan. But hold on, don't mind me gassing away.
Let me ask you one of my questions. Your father was a
Derry man?

Johnny He was certainly. Apprentice Boys, siege of Derry,
history of tempest and discord. Old days. (*Nothing
for a little.*) The ragged trousers . . . bones in the stew,
good Northern cabbage from the farm, where the slugs
disported themselves. Hearth of the cricket, the zinc
bucket by the door, muslin, summer heat, the black
boatmen skittering about, a mirror for a young face,
a cold mirror from the bowels of the earth.

Aisling Sounds very – colourful.

Johnny Oh? (*A moment.*) No. Poor. You know.

Aisling Oh.

*Stephen comes in with some things on a tray, just cups
and so on. No teapot as yet.*

Stephen Ah, the old topic. Rich men and their childhood
poverty.

Aisling smiles politely.

Johnny Stephen, she is not interested in your banter.

Stephen Excuse me, Mr Silvester. I was thinking aloud.

Poised, doing nothing. Johnny gives him a look.

I'll get the teapot. Just drawing. (*He goes.*)

Aisling He does say strange things.

Johnny Does he? Poverty. But the heart is neither rich
nor poor. I must lie down where all the – somethings
start, in the foul rag-and-bone shop of the heart. Yeats,
you know.

Aisling Oh, yes.

Johnny I would spread my cloak under your feet, if it were only the breadth of a farthing. The salmon, the elk, the bull, the wren on the farthing. Such pretty coins. (*A moment.*) Did Stephen bring some tea?

Aisling shakes her head.

I had about three hundred cousins in Derry when I was a little boy. We knew them all. In and out of the house. Not all at the one time. (*A moment, very gracious, meek.*) Left when I was five. Packed up our few sticks, headed South. (*A moment.*) Derry. Hinterland. Haunted terrain. You have read your Heaney? *North*? Perfection. The griddle iron, a plaque of heat against the wall. Peeling spuds with his ma. Kavanagh too, the master. Similar vein. Makes you proud to be Irish. My black hills have never seen the sun rising, eternally they look North towards Armagh. You would die for those poems.

Aisling Hold on a sec, Mr Silvester. (*holding her stomach*) I'm afraid I guzzled a sausage at breakfast. Dear me. (*recovering*) Well, I don't need to slavishly follow these? (*her notes*) I can extemporise. That's what gets the best results. Not that I've tackled a living subject before. But you know, one has an instinct for these things. I think I might make a marvellous actress, but then, lawyers earn a fortune. I'll get back on track. As a contrast to the poverty you spoke about, your Derry family, you have a private jet, don't you? Could your father have imagined such a thing?

Johnny Well, he was sick, you see, unwell.

Aisling And would . . .

Johnny A dark mirror.

Aisling I'm sorry?

Johnny Such sickness. Time sweeps everything away, nothing left, who cares now besides myself what he was,

53

what he said, the sorrow that came to him? (*A moment.*) If you want the little luxuries of life . . . In fact, the story of the jet is – well, I don't know if funny is the word. Because I am not a rich man, Aisling. I have seen very little money in my time. Held it in my hand. Money is a state of mind. Modern money exists philosophically. (*A moment.*) May I illustrate? It is not the domestic history of Derry, as such. It is just my history.

Aisling Oh, please. It will lighten my task, you see.

Johnny Well, I have a phone in my car that is paid for by the state. This concession is linked to a larger group of concessions, except the other things I never utilise. So they appear as zeros on the accounts, which people like. There was, until recently, an understanding that occasional exceptional spending might also go on this bill, and it was accepted that these things might now and then be quite large, especially when I was head of the country. This arrangement reached into an account I held as a partner in a dairy farm enterprise in the midlands, that supplied an enormous quantity of milk into the European surplus, and in recognition of this the Central Milk Board allowed the company a concession of three per cent on every second container of milk that went into intervention. This money was computed as a boon to the Irish economy and therefore enshrined more or less in a larger body of funds directly enhanced by the state at quarterly intervals. Out of this I paid my expenses *vis-à-vis* my private jet. Therefore the position was that my private jet was paid for ultimately by the mobile phone. You see? It is all innocent enough. I keep telling them that. Modernity.

Aisling It is still – a form of poverty, on a grand scale.

Johnny That's what we used to call at the university a brilliant remark. What is the subject of your thesis, Aisling?

Aisling Thesis? Oh, God. It's not a thesis. I'm just an undergraduate. It's a term paper.

Johnny A term paper? Stephen gets everything a little – skewed. I will remonstrate with him. Misinformation, the triumph of the twentieth century. Oh, well. Never mind.

Aisling I'm sorry if you think you were misled.

Stephen comes in with the silver teapot.

Johnny No, no. Oh, thank you, Stephen, very welcome.

Stephen hands tea to Johnny, then to Aisling.

Stephen (*the teapot*) He gave the sister of that one to Mrs Thatcher. They were a pair. The teapots were, I mean. No disrespect. (*A moment, Johnny almost sullen.*) Alright, Miss?

Aisling Yes.

Stephen They feed you properly at the university?

Aisling (*surprised*) Yes.

Stephen nods sagely.

Johnny TV crew all packed up?

Stephen Only a memory now, sir.

Suddenly Jack appears in the door. The others look at him.

Jack Oh – sorry, Daddy. I was just wanting to talk to you. About last night.

Johnny That's alright, Jack. We can talk later.

Jack walks in, quite close to Aisling, not threatening.

Jack Who are you?

Aisling Aisling, I'm Aisling.

55

Jack Oh, *you're* Aisling. I see. (*smiling*)

Johnny I tell you what, Jack. Pop back in a while, eh?

Jack Alright. Alright. I'll – circle, in the garden, like an airplane.

Stephen Why not? Good for you. Put on your anorak – it's cold out there.

Jack goes.

Aisling Who was that?

Johnny No one. My son.

Stephen (*to Aisling*) Biscuit?

She's not heeding him.

I said, biscuit?

She looks at him.

Marietta? Kimberley? Fig-roll? McDonagh's Digestive? Dunk?

Aisling Oh, no, never – since childhood.

Stephen I know what you mean. Nothing tastes as it did when we were little ones, does it? Marietta dunked in your tea – now there was a treat. Ambrosia. Or manna even, that nourished the Israelites.

Johnny Thank you very much, Stephen.

Stephen senses the dismissal. Goes.

I'm a little tired after the television interview. Long night. Wandering the house.

Aisling I'm sorry it's only a term paper. Oh, but my father is a lecturer at the University, in Galway. Someday I will tackle the doctorate, I'm sure, if I stick to the studies.

Johnny It doesn't matter. Galway – they never offered me an honorary doctorate, you know. I think they might have. I would have thought my achievements merited that.

Aisling That's not what my father says, but let's leave him out of it.

Johnny Oh, let's not. Let's include him. What does he say about me then?

Aisling I don't know. He just goes blathering on, you know.

Johnny But what does he say?

Aisling He has strong opinions on just about everything.

Johnny Such as?

Aisling I think he feels that, with all the tribunals, you know, something has been lost. I don't know if you'd agree with that.

His face.

Probably not. But I'm not here for, you know, current affairs, I'm here for history.

Johnny Your father is entitled to his opinion. Academia, the last refuge of the scoundrel.

Aisling My father is a good, decent person, I have to say. As fathers go.

Johnny His grasp of political science may be weak, nonetheless.

Aisling He's a lecturer in Modern Irish History.

Johnny Well, there you are. Revisionism.

Aisling Scholarship boy, books, youngest chair in the history of the department, all that jazz.

Johnny To quote another of our Irish writers, Mr Brendan Behan, Esquire, tolerable house-painter and dramatist of genius, 'Fuck the bedgrudgers.'

Aisling (*laughing*) Well, he would say that. But, it's odd to hear you saying that. I thought you'd be too straight-laced now for a remark like that.

Johnny It's a literary quotation. (*A moment, sunken again.*) I'm tired of the outpourings of men like your father. They speak, they write, and they do not know what they do to me. They are killing me, in effect.

Aisling He doesn't really wish you any harm. Not personally. But please, Mr Silvester, let's get off this topic.

Johnny I know what I'm talking about. As I am on the receiving end of their wisdom. I don't know your father. But I don't have to know him to imagine the sort of scurrilous intimations he may be fond of promulgating.

Aisling Hold your horses, Mr Silvester.

Johnny What?

Aisling Steady on, I mean. (*pulling out some cuttings*) Listen to what this fella says about you in the *Irish Times*, if you think my father's bad.

Johnny Please, spare me.

Aisling 'Far from adding lustre to the country he claims to have served, he has brought it low in the estimation of the nations.'

Johnny Oh, for God's sake.

Aisling 'His grimy manoeuvrings are tied at his heels now like a gaggle of tin cans, that rattle wherever he goes.' My father's opinions are friendly by comparison, believe me.

Johnny Atrocious nonsense!

Aisling I just had it in my bag here, part of my research. Frankly, I think the world's gone mad. One opinion madder than the next.

Johnny Sometimes I would like to take the lot of them out into a yard and shoot them, like General Maxwell in 1916. It would be nice to have it out with them. Hah? Definitively.

Aisling Have it out with me, if you want to. I'm not afraid of debate.

Johnny This is not a little college debating society. This is my life, my home, my heart.

Aisling You know, you're not accused by begrudgers, really, but the people that loved you. I suppose that's worse. My father used to think you were a hero, a political genius.

Johnny Well, that's better. That's good news.

Aisling He doesn't any more, alas. I'm afraid he feels betrayed, greatly betrayed.

Johnny You're subtle. You're kind, but you are like a dagger. Look, I made this country. How you live, how you are, the clothes on your pretty back, even your damned confusion in the face of reality – you owe it all to me. I made you, Aisling Dwyer. I asked the hard questions long ago. The father of the nation. Do you understand? (*A moment.*) I have the whole country against me now. Do you know what that's like? They will never understand. It's because they're comfortable, afflicted by comfort. It has softened their brains. No one remembers the hard days. Derry made me, Dublin undid me.

Aisling Hmm, but you're wrong, Mr Silvester.

Johnny Hah?

Aisling You didn't make me, did you? My father made me, of course, and my mother. I don't mean to be unfair. I want to say things to you without fear, that are true and just. I tell you what you've given me, Mr Silvester – shame, I'm afraid. Shame when I read articles about you, and your friends and associates. You are comfortable too, comfortable and at ease about your acts and monuments. I mean, you did enrich yourself, you allowed those men in their expensive suits to give you those quiet millions, you surrounded yourself with this amazing house. Some people would love to see you go to prison, you know.

Johnny Of course I know!

Aisling It's all very odd. Where are the good men? I do not know. Where in the world would you find politicians that have an inner sense of political, political *love*, of moral grandeur that comes from having, from having nothing?

Johnny I don't know, Aisling.

Aisling The funny thing is, I love my country.

Johnny The funny thing is, I do too.

Aisling Boy, have we drifted. Domestic history of Derry, how are you?

Johnny (*after a moment, blankly, staring at her*) What? What did you say? Exhaustion. You asked me something? I asked you? I don't remember. Old. You see. Blood slows in the veins. Beauty an affront. I pass mere street kids in the city, going by in my car, shouting, God knows, dealing in drugs, abused, beaten by the guards, who knows – but young. Oh Jack, Jack. I would change places with any of them. Let them have the house, the fields, the car, the damned jet. But youth – gone, unreachable, loveliness, no more, soft hands, debarred.

Aisling looking at him.

Not entirely well. (*tearful. After a little*) I, I. Exhaustion. Years. My son . . .

Aisling (*after a moment, puzzled, softly*) Are you . . . crying, Mr Silvester?

Johnny No, dust in the eye, old plaster. Ceiling. Hints of the past, that powerful hinterland. Strange.

Aisling (*a moment*) I'm sorry.

He breaks down into sobs. She awkwardly puts a hand on his arm. He grips it powerfully, sobbing. She tries to draw away.

Aisling Can you let my hand go, there's a good man?

Johnny Nothing – nothing!

Aisling (*loudly*) Can you let go, please?

Stephen comes in immediately.

Stephen Ah ha, ah ha.

Johnny God give me strength.

Stephen (*unlocking Johnny's fingers one by one with difficulty*) Oh, rapscallion. There now, Mr Silvester. Let her go. Eeny, meeny, miny, mo. Let her go. (*He succeeds.*)

Aisling (*to Stephen*) I've upset him. I didn't take into account his – his age. He really is an old man. Is he alright? He seems to wander a lot in his talk.

Stephen He's ding-dong, perfecto. Never you mind. Let me assist you. Let me give you your coat in the hall. Let me show you to the door. Did you get some good material?

Aisling I've no idea.

Stephen Well, anyway. Let's just slip out, you and me. He'll be fine in a minute. Very stressful days. Son not the best. Phone call. Blackrock Clinic. Weight of public opinion. A ruined man. Was so admired, now, in some quarters so reviled. Hurts him terribly. Appearance of . . .

Aisling Oh God. Well, I have added to his store of hurt then.

Stephen Best to go, best to go.

Aisling I think so. (*Stands with her possessions gathered up a moment.*) Goodbye, Mr Silvester. I'm very, very sorry. Goodbye.

No answer. She goes out with Stephen.

Johnny (*a moment, in a low growl, then with growing venom*) God call down upon them all a filthy plague, may their bodies riot with disease, their guts churn with odious micro-organisms, their limbs break out with weeping pustules, a tarry bile pour down upon their heads –

Bang of front door.

– their most cherished plans turn to bitter gall, their marriages end in murderous recriminations, their hearts fester with resentment and cholesterol!

Stephen (*returning*) Cup of tea, Mr Silvester?

Johnny (*after a moment of reflection*) That would be most welcome.

Stephen Right.

Johnny If she says anything to Daisy I think I will hang myself.

Stephen Oh, don't worry, Mr Silvester, about that young woman.

Johnny No?

Stephen No. Don't worry. Put it out of your mind.

Johnny Thank you, Stephen.

Stephen You're welcome.

Johnny I should have thrown her out on her pretty ear. Even to sit rowing a few moments with beauty . . .

Stephen Mr Achilles's weakness.

Johnny (*gently*) Fuck off, Stephen.

Stephen goes. A moment.

There's nothing for me now, only the dreary fight, the justification, the resistance, and maybe utter disgrace, loneliness, prison, privations which I cannot imagine. In prison, alone, sick, suffering . . . Maybe I can imagine it! Cornelius!

Cornelius enters quietly. Johnny registers him.

I hope you haven't come back in here to torment me, Cornelius Ryan. (*After a moment, with force, striking the desk.*) You'd think I had established some kind of terrible South American regime! If people are free to criticise me, without getting their throats cut, or disappeared in some damn football stadium, some Croke Park, if the future is wondrously bright, if the present itself is a bed of excellent roses, if an Irish citizen knows their sons and daughters can remain close-by, and grandchildren no longer be the subject of photographs and long-distant longing, then, Cornelius, there is in my story some not inconsiderable glory! And some thanks due to me, Cornelius! (*After a moment.*) I love my son.

I love my country. But the sad fact is, I must conclude, that love is no defence. (*A moment.*) What can I do? Where can I go, Cornelius?

Cornelius What are you getting at, Johnny?

Johnny I'll stay here, I suppose, in my disgrace. Is it such an ignoble condition, if conjoined with silence?

Cornelius Who said that, Johnny?

Johnny I did, Cornelius.

Cornelius It was well said. I think the Irish people would enjoy your silence.

Johnny They'll have it, shortly, maybe. Dr fucking Cunningham. Back and forward in my mind, life, death, death, life. It's worse than waiting for election results. No news is . . . a pain in the arse. (*A moment.*) I suppose you're familiar with this particular street of fear, old friend?

Cornelius No street on earth is bleaker, darker. (*quoting*) And I never will return again for to plough the Rocks of Bawn . . . (*smiling*) I have to be off, Johnny. I hope I have done you some service. State of grace?

Johnny Come on, come on, let us have no bullshit now, here at the edge of the world, for God's sake. Alright. When the hunger-strikers started to die, one by one, falling like rooks from a tree in a terrible frost, I knew my heart was compromised. I felt my father turning – painfully – in his grave. Come on, come on, Cornelius. How many times did you lift the edge of the carpet, and let me sweep the dust under it? Fellas like you, fellas like me, Cornelius, cannot expect monuments erected to our piety. Have a heart. Look it, look it, I loved you dearly. I can say no more.

Cornelius (*a moment*) Alright, Johnny. Maybe it was all worth it anyhow. Your arm raised in victory was sweet to me. Even in defeat, what was defeat? A million pieces of buttered toast, a thousand gallons of scalding tea. The damp villages of Ireland. The locals taking us to their hearts, amazed we had gone to the trouble of visiting them under the rain. You and me, shaking hands, and telling stories after in the back of the Merc, the rain dribbling down the windows, and us laughing, laughing. Bless me, Johnny, you were the good companion. (*A moment.*) You won't see me again. But I am only a shadow man.

Johnny (*not facing him, looking out the window*) What a pity love is no defence. What a tragedy.

Cornelius We're only an upright ape, standing on our back legs trying to reach the higher apples. You can't expect too much of such a creature.

Cornelius is gone.

Johnny You're a good man, Cornelius, that's your problem.

Johnny goes and sits at his desk, back to the door, breathing quietly. Behind him, Jack comes to the door, clears his throat. He's dressed in his anorak.

(*Without turning around*) Go away, Cornelius, for God's sake. I hate a man that says he is going and then doesn't go. Like Senator Moynihan that time, when the shit hit the fan for the umpteenth time. And he came into my new office in Government Buildings, covered in all that lovely wood panelling – for the greater glory of Ireland, mind – and he spoke to me in what he imagined was his gentlemanly way, in truth berating me and withdrawing his craven support during the vote of confidence. Then he turns to go and I look down at my papers, allowing him only a brief goodbye. I was disgusted by him. A minute later I look up and the bugger is still in the room. 'What the hell are you still doing here?' I said. 'I can't find the door,' he says, 'in all this panelling.' 'Well,' says I, 'why don't you fuck yourself out the window?'

Jack Daddy?

Johnny Oh, Jack, sorry.

Jack I was looking for you. Circling, circling.

Johnny I'm here just.

Jack To explain . . .

They stare at each other. Quite a long pause.

If possible . . . to restore . . .

Johnny (*kindly*) What, Jack?

Jack struggling to speak, then just struggling, distressed.

You took your tablets? You have that glazed . . . (*He looks away, head goes down.*)

Jack What's the matter, Daddy?

Johnny (*despite himself*) I hate when you call me Daddy. Why not Dad, or Da, or something more Irish, like? Never mind.

Jack I am sorry you have so much to . . .

Johnny Thank you. I appreciate your – solicitude. I am – overwhelmed . . .

Jack Prozac or something – might help – that's what they give the sad men in John of God's.

Johnny What? (*A moment.*) It's not the old head, Jack.

Phone ringing. Johnny lets it a moment, staring at his son.

66

Excuse me, Jack. (*He lifts it.*) Yes? – Hello? – What? (*harshly*) Jesus, you have the balls of a brass monkey, woman! I know you rang yesterday, I'm very aware of it. I said then I had nothing to say to you. Yes, yes, alright, I am unwell, in fact, in fact, I have died. Goodbye! (*Slams down phone. It starts to ring again.*) Have they no mercy? (*Hauls up the receiver.*) In the name of Jesus, can you not leave me alone? (*softly*) Oh, Dr Cunningham. (*listening*) I see. I see. Oh. (*A long moment, breathing, head down.*) That's – thank you. Thank you, Doctor. Thank you for ringing. Yes. Goodbye now. (*Puts down phone.*)

Jack What, Daddy?

Daisy busily comes in.

Daisy We're off to cousin Aggie's, Johnny.

Johnny (*as if cheerily*) Of course you are!

Jack The doctor just rang.

Daisy (*not hearing him, to Johnny*) Do you want to come with us?

Johnny (*brightly*) No, no, sure I'll linger on here.

Daisy How did the interview with the young woman go?

Johnny West, I fear. But west is, is good!

Daisy She was very complimentary about you to Stephen, Stephen says. A great statesman, she called you.

Johnny Good, good. Good for Stephen. You know, I think I'll go to my bed. And sleep for a week. And awake like Rip Van Winkle in a fresh new world.

Daisy Well, don't forget our trip next week. Paris. Josephine's garden.

Johnny Oh, yes? You think it a good notion? You have mulled it over. And, a positive outcome. Oh, splendid, Daisy, dear. Excellent, Daisy, excellent! I will mark it in my diary. A joy in the offing. We'll sail off together, you, me, and Jack. We can't leave out Jack!

Daisy Alright. We'll see you in a few days, Johnny.

Johnny Of course, Daisy. See you.

He looks up at her. She smiles.

Daisy (*puzzled by him*) Hmmm. You'll be alright here with Stephen?

Johnny I will say my prayers and think my thoughts. God is good.

Daisy Come on, Jack. We'll leave your father to his – work. The car is waiting.

Jack The doctor just rang.

Daisy Oh?

Jack Bye, Da.

Jack embraces him awkwardly.

Johnny (*awkwardly*) Bye, Jack. Bye.

Jack goes.

Good boy.

Daisy You are – alright, aren't you? Chipper enough?

Johnny Ding-dong. Perfecto. The doctor did just ring, actually.

Daisy Oh? Good news?

Johnny (*a moment, then smiling*) Yes. Of course. Best.

Daisy I'm pleased. (*She comes back and kisses him.*) New days then. I was worried about you, oddly enough. I'm – relieved.

Johnny Yes. It is a relief.

Daisy And I am touched by your offer to go to France with me.

Johnny (*a moment*) When was the last time anyway that I said I loved you, Daisy? As a matter of record, as we used to say in the Dail.

Daisy Don't know. Nineteen eighty-four?

Johnny I could say it now easily if you like, and mean it. If I had your approbation, I could endure anything. (*moved*) You were beautiful in your youth, Daisy, and you still are. We'll go about. We'll make a habit of it. We'll see all the gardens of France together. Every last one!

Daisy (*coming closer*) Alright, Johnny. One garden at a time will do.

Touching his face. He smiles.

Johnny (*joking*) Don't hit me now. Oh, hit me if you like!

But Daisy leans forward and kisses his cheek.

Daisy I'm sorry for some of the hard things I've said to you. There is a fine man in you. Just as good as my father. And a tender man. I know. I do still love you, Johnny. Hence all the pain.

Johnny I am grateful, Daisy. For the opportunity to say also, I do love you. I most certainly do love you, and apologise . . .

Daisy Alright. It's settled. We will strike forward, Johnny. And look after Jack. And all the things.

Johnny definitely moved. He is marooned by the feeling. Daisy smiles at him.

Johnny (*a moment*) Listen, have a good time at ould cousin Aggie's. Have a ball.

Daisy goes out. For a little, Johnny stands listening. The taxi going off. He returns to his desk and takes up the letter again.

Johnny Dear Aunts Winnie and Beatrice,
I hope you are both well, as I am well. I am thinking of you both today, thinking of the old days when I was young among you, and you prized me so greatly just for being a boy. The luxury and happiness of that. I am sorry it is so long since I wrote. But often and often my mind goes back to the haven of your Derry farm, the ordered yard, the hens all neurotic in the evenings, the beautiful bread baked in the pot-oven set between the flags, the great hoard of hay in the high barn, the warm little bellies of the freshly laid eggs, and all the wonders and exceptionalities of that world. And I want to thank you even so late as this for all that bliss, when my father your brother was still strong and lively, and carried me on his shoulders across the summer meadow infected with every wild flower known to that gay and solemn kingdom, the hinterland of Derry. I thank you, dear aunts, and hope to make the journey north to see you soon, especially now in these fresh times of peace so welcome and so long worked for.
Your loving and grateful nephew,
John.

He sits there a while.

P.S. It is the anniversary today of Beatrice, little Betty to you and me. May God rest her.

He stands and gazes out of the window, thinking. At length he sees someone outside. A hint of panic.

Not here, not now.

He goes out urgently.

What are you thinking of, Connie? What are you doing here?

Sound of front door (off). At length he leads back in a woman in her fifties, hair dyed dark, tanned, with a short skirt not unlike the young woman's earlier, half concealed in a long fashionable yellow coat.

Connie I was driving home across the Phoenix Park and heard the four o'clock news headlines on the car radio. What a jolt. It said it had been confirmed that you were unwell, that you had seen a doctor in the Blackrock Clinic and were definitely unwell.

Johnny Monstrous!

Connie I tried to reach you discreetly on my mobile, but, dear, how many times have you changed your number? It is impossible to reach you.

Johnny (*smiling*) And you call yourself a journalist.

Connie But is it true? I drove straight over. I waited outside the gates across the road under the willow trees like long ago, and saw Daisy and Jack drive out at last. I spoke to the Special Branch man and though he didn't know me, he had heard of me at any rate, and allowed me to enter the grounds.

Johnny Of course he knew you, Connie. Haven't you sold what you call your bloody story, which is in fact my story, to every newspaper in the land? What were you thinking of?

Connie But, dear, you rang me that night and were so cruel, so harsh, so sudden. Cutting me off from you. Just terrible. What was I to do? Sit at home gaping out the window at the Phoenix Monument? A girl has to make a living somehow.

Johnny Anyway it doesn't matter now. It is done. Connie, I don't want you here. I don't want to see you. Daisy has just gone out for an hour to see a friend.

Connie Now, you will have to do better than that. The Special Branch man told me everything. Cousin Aggie till the weekend. Just like old times.

Johnny It is immaterial. Alright, you are too clever for me. You always were.

Connie Well, I tried to educate you, darling. All those books. The gloss of culture at least. Quotations! Never the real thing perhaps, but a most effective and beautiful imitation.

Johnny I am so glad I don't have to listen to this any more. I am so glad I am too old to listen to it. All that old Connie gabble. I adored it once, I am sure.

Connie You adored everything, dear. Perhaps you still might? (*She shows the side of her leg under the coat.*)

Johnny (*turning his back to her*) What was pleasing and attractive in youth is often simply grotesque in late middle age, don't you think?

Connie You cruel bastard.

Johnny I've had enough of ladies in short skirts today.

Connie Oh. Lucky you. But, Johnny, I haven't come to have an old-fashioned row. Oh, beauty has faded and her charms are no more. I was moved by the broadcast. I was crying in the car. The view of the president's gates as I passed was suddenly blurry. Are you really not well?

Johnny I'm perfectly fine and I want you to go. We sorted all this out on the telephone. You were not to contact me again. And here you are in person, with a short skirt and a long coat. For God's sake, Connie. I am grateful for your concern, of course. Thank you. But there's nothing in it. A rumour, like all the other rumours.

Connie As far as I know, none of the other things are rumours really, but facts.

Johnny Please, Connie, please, just go back out the way you came.

Connie We were as good as man and wife for thirty years, Johnny.

Johnny Daisy is my wife. You were not my wife.

Connie What was I then? Put a name on it.

Johnny Someone I loved, someone I inconveniently and probably immorally loved.

Connie Immorally. Hmm. Maybe so. But such wonderful journeys together. In European trains. Couchettes. The drumming of the carriages through the Alps, the South of France, the food, the wine, the nights, the stars, the bloody love I had for you and you for me.

Johnny Of course.

Connie The bloody first-class, world-beating, out-and-out, sensational mind-blowing sex. The seventies, Johnny, the eighties, when you and I were in our prime. I admit, the old sides have plumped out, the arse has slightly fallen, and that's just you, as the fella said. Look what's happened to me. Even a short skirt can't make you lose your mind, forget your responsibilities to family and nation. Ah, those were the days, Johnny.

Johnny Those *were* the days. And I still have the highest regard for you. You upset me with your scandalous outpourings, but you have spirit, real spirit, and in your youth, beauty to burn. But it is all old chapters of a lost book, Connie. And I urgently need you to go now.

Connie You are quite well then?

Johnny I am beleaguered but in reasonable form.

Connie Of course you are beleaguered. They're really going to get you, aren't they? I'm sorry.

Johnny Going to? They're *out* to get me. Whether they do is another matter. Now, Connie.

Connie Of course I'll go. I just had to come over. Be assured of my continued – love, Johnny. Don't think of us as tawdry or immoral, is that the word you used? (*coming close to him, neutral, a hand on his arm*) We were meant to be together.

Johnny Maybe so. Long ago. But it has caused such pain.

Connie Johnny, I know you're in the shit. But I feel so old, so hated, so diminished.

Johnny Don't feel those things, my dear. Rise up, lovely Connie, and give your horse some hay . . . (*his hand briefly on hers, smiling*)

Connie (*smiling*) I don't suppose there will be an end to this – some time of respite?

Johnny Well, Connie, we Irish like to kill our kings when they get old. Next year it all starts again. I will gather what's left of my strength to withstand them. And you must try to do the same. Please go now, Connie.

Connie (*going*) There were only ever two women in your life, Johnny. I think that is a good score for a modern European gentleman.

Johnny (*smiling*) I don't know what to say to that.

Connie (*a moment, her old poise.*) See you round, dear. (*She begins to go.*)

Lights and noise of car entering the gates beyond in the twilight. Johnny looks at Connie.

Johnny Ford Cortina, 1978? I hope and pray. How are you on the engines, Connie?

The car drawing up on the gravel outside. He goes to window.

Oh, Christ. Get down out of sight, they're back.

Connie Who is?

Johnny Daisy and Jack. Oh, please disappear, Connie. I'll open the window when they come in the hall and you can jump out.

Connie Johnny, don't ask me to jump out the window.

Johnny Why not?

Connie You lame fool of a man, this is a Gandon house, this is a sprung floor, we're seven feet up in the air here, I know what I'm talking about.

Johnny I knew that *Irish Homes and Gardens* would have a deleterious effect on Irish life . . . Christ Almighty, get in there and be quiet.

He is putting her into the State Papers cupboard, pulling papers out and stacking them hurriedly on his desk.

Connie (*indignant*) In here? This is not a bedroom farce, Johnny.

Johnny Well, this is not a bedroom, it is a State Papers cupboard.

He closes over the doors. Composes himself.

They mightn't come in here anyway, please God. (*He listens.*)

Daisy and Jack come in.

Daisy Sorry, Johnny, to disturb you. Jack forgot his Walkman. He thinks he might have left it in here. Did you see it?

Johnny Oh – no. I don't think so. I don't think it's in here, Jack.

Jack Oh, okay, Daddy. (*nervously*) Dad. Da. (*to Daisy*) I can't, Mam, I can't leave without it.

Johnny Horrible traffic all down the country at this hour. Kinnegad will be a nightmare. But if you set off now you might miss the worst of it.

Daisy Alright. Come on then, Jack. We can make do with the car radio.

Johnny Very good.

They're going.

Bon voyage now. Have a nice time.

Jack (*turning*) Oh, I remember, Daddy!

Johnny Hah?

Jack Remember? The beef. (*Goes towards the cupboard.*)

Johnny gently tries to prevent him. Jack smilingly goes past.

It's okay, Daddy.

He opens the doors. There's Connie, holding the Walkman.

Connie (*to Jack*) Is that what you wanted?

Jack astonished. Daisy stands looking at her. Suddenly she starts to cry.

Connie Oh, Daisy, I'm terribly sorry.

Daisy Don't speak to me in my own house!

Connie It's not what it looks. I didn't intend to sneak in, it just happened. The Special Branch man let me in. I heard the news on the radio and had to come over.

Daisy What news?

Johnny Apparently it was reported on the four o'clock that I am unwell. Misinformation!

Connie So it is all quite innocent.

Daisy He would hardly have put you in a cupboard if it was quite innocent.

Jack (*incoherently*) I did not want, I did not want . . .

Johnny But it is, Daisy.

Daisy This is the last betrayal, Johnny. I will stand no more of it. You just lie and lie and lie. (*Silence.*) Jack, get your Walkman if it is so important to your state of mind. Come along.

Connie I was just going, Daisy.

Jack Daddy, I know this woman. I met her with you. Train station, when I was seventeen. 'You are a man of the world, Jack,' you said. 'Don't mention this to your mother.' And I did not know what you meant. I did not want . . .

Daisy Johnny, how could you do this? Are you such a great fool after all? Josephine's garden . . .

Connie Oh, outside Paris?

Daisy Shut up, you stupid, stupid woman!

Connie (*bursting into tears herself*) I'm sorry, I'm sorry. This is horrible!

Daisy The contempt you must have for me, creeping into my house like this. You don't understand women like me. We love more deeply, we understand things that you . . . (*fiercely*) I hope you have read your Dante, and are looking forward to your fate in the lower circle of hell.

Connie Dante, my lovely backside.

Daisy Destructive, pathetic, alien woman.

Connie (*defiantly*) I gave him fun, gaiety and good times, what did you give him? Dreary, old . . .

Daisy Look at you, standing in the State Papers cupboard, trying vainly to insult me!

Johnny Connie, don't attack the woman in her own house, please.

Daisy Oh, fuck you too – the both of you!

Jack I did not want, I did not want to be complicit!

Suddenly Jack rushes at his father. The two fall to the ground. Jack is on top and is punching him weakly.

Connie (*horrified*) Oh, dear. Oh, dear.

Daisy Jack!

The two women hurry over and ease Jack off his father.

Daisy You just can't do that, Jack . . .

Connie Oh dear, oh dear . . .

Jack is crying. Neither helps Johnny up. They stand there in a clump of humanity. Stephen hurries in.

Stephen Intruders? The window-catch?

Johnny (*from the ground*) Singular, Stephen. Intruder.

Stephen Were you assaulted?

78

Johnny Not at all.

Stephen (*accusingly*) I don't know why you've been left lying on the ground.

Daisy Because he is a contemptible liar.

Stephen He may have his faults, Mrs Silvester, but he is no liar. If you will forgive me for saying so.

Daisy I think I know my husband better than you, Stephen.

Stephen I know you do, well, I know you do. Because I am only a – factotum.

Johnny You are a personal assistant. And on that note, would you mind, Stephen, bringing this lady out to the gates, of your kindness?

Connie This lady? (*A moment.*) I *am* sorry, Daisy Silvester, I don't care what you say back. (*Daisy doesn't answer.*) He has no one to help him up now except that old man. Johnny Silvester, the poor archangel.

She goes with Stephen.

Stephen (*as he goes, to Connie*) You have no business to be calling me an old man.

Daisy (*a moment*) How lovely it all is.

Johnny I'm sorry, but, it was not my doing, I assure you.

Daisy Not your doing? Why does that have a familiar ring?

Johnny It was a mere error. Connie just turned up. I had no hand or part in it. I swear.

Daisy Excrement. You manufacture a sort of moral excrement, that flies everywhere. To have released again a kind of love, only for it to be thrown back at me.

Johnny Now, Daisy. Mercy. Think of our plans.

Daisy Mercy? I have no grudge against her, although I would gladly run her over with a steamroller. But you, you half-hearted man, with your long serious face, your stupidity all dressed up to look like intelligence, you have my eternal contempt. Jack, go and fetch that Walkman.

Jack goes and takes the Walkman and holds it, head bowed.

Jack Chapelizod Bridge, the whale, the man crushed in his bubble-car. Then old Moby Dick drifted out to sea. The Irish Sea swallowed the Great White Whale. And that was the end of the story. Oh Lordy, trouble so hard, oh Lordy.

Johnny Jack?

Jack (*turning to him, clear*) Beyond belief. Beyond redemption. A creature to frighten a child in a fairy tale. The pooka himself. All the words I hear. You are – not – a proper man. Not a good father. Not a good man. I am sorrowing.

Daisy brings him to the door, he goes out.

Johnny (*appalled*) Sorrowing.

Daisy looks at him.

Johnny Where are you going to go, Daisy?

Daisy Cousin Aggie's. As planned.

Johnny Look it, this has been a curious day. Don't go to cousin Aggie's. Stay, and we'll thrash it out.

Daisy Ordinary, decent cousin Aggie in Mullingar, who will make room for me and Jack in her hospitable and honourable house.

Johnny I can't bear it, Daisy. This time, I swear it on my father's grave, Connie just turned up. (*A moment.*)

Okay, go to Aggie's, a time of respite, but what then, what then?

Daisy You'll be hearing what then, in due course. My God, Johnny – oh, never mind. How could I explain it to you? Another planet, like you said. The sad, hot, little planet of the damned.

Johnny (*hopelessly, almost to himself, with heavy pain*) Have you no sense of humour, Daisy? Because, here is the joke. I am falsely accused.

Daisy You, a little man, given a last chance. Oh, I know what awaits me. I know the nature of my own sentence well enough. And Jack's. But you – I can see you in this house in ten years' time, when old age has got a proper grip of you. When it will finally have sunk in, what you are, what you have done. The great iron hammer of guilt that will smash down on your despicable, eternal self-regard. And you will be a nightmare figure in this ruined house. With filthy hair and withered body, the lonely pooka-man of Ireland. And not one moment of pity for you will register in the annals of humankind. You have earned all our contempt and hatred. God Himself will reject you. Even the devil may scorn to have you in his fearsome halls!

They're gone.

Johnny Daisy!

Listening. The noises of the doors. The car starting, driving off. Pain in his face.

Oh, Lordy, the trouble I've seen . . .

Differently, a real prayer. Cornelius appears quietly, watching.

Oh, Lord, look down upon your excremental being, for he knows what he has done. Forgive him, restore him,

81

and let him go. Innocence or guilt, it is all the one.
(*A moment.*) Jack. (*A moment.*) Such a sight to gaze on!
The nurse said, 'Look, Mr Silvester, he is pinkening.'
I had never heard the word. A new-born child, slowly
gaining colour. Pinkening. Passion! From there to here.
Not a good man. (*A moment, very simply.*) But, I love
him. Not a good man. But, I love.

> *Cornelius quietly withdrawing. A moment, getting*
> *himself up with difficulty.*

Never, never, never, never, never. (*After a moment.*)
That's not Milton, is it, Connie? That way madness lies.
Never explain, never say you're sorry. (*After a moment,*
with courage.) Do not give way to regret . . .

> *He slowly circles the room, looking at the paraphernalia*
> *of his career, beginning to touch things, statuettes,*
> *citations, running his fingers along the spines of*
> *his expensive books, like a child with a stick on a*
> *railing.*

I'll resist. I'll do as I have always done. I'll be that tiger
tiger burning bright in the forest of the night.

> *He pulls a few things down, throws them on the desk.*

If they want a great national criminal, here I am.
Here I am, you fettered cunts, do your worst, you
dreary pack of civil service dogs. I'm Johnny Silvester.
There would have been no modern era, no change,
no new world without me. Alright, you safe little
badgers in your suburban sets, there has been a price,
I see that. I am the giant of the modern era. The age
of Silvester will take up many a chapter in the history
of Ireland. Whatever you do to me now, no one can
erase me, no one can destroy the old films of my doings,
no one can silence the fucking birdsong I will leave
behind me. I will give you nothing, you neutered spaniels.

I will make you fight every inch of any indictment against me.

He pulls out the remaining papers and throws them roughly on the desk, making a snowy heap. He climbs on to the desk.

I will smile and smile and be a holy villain. I will outlast your hunger for revenge, and survive to a time when the people will understand me again, as having worked for them in the upshot. And they will send their good words and everything will be as before, the beautiful handshakes in country towns, the hospitality inside the rain. Because they will know that I blackened my heart and soul for them. Let no one say I started out an idealist, no, I was a savage from the start. I will make a great stride like a giant in one of Jack's storybooks years ago, and cross all these troubles like a ditch, like a Monaghan dyke. There is something of Jekyll and Hyde in us all, my little judges, let him who is without sin . . . I will convert my heart into a great secret and hide there, and sortie out like old Geronimo in the last days of the West, and crush your houses with their exhausted gardens, and devour your resolve, and melt it into terror. I will outlast you, turning your admired middle age into the addled decrepitude and loneliness of the old! I will live, I will live for ever, like a fucking vampire!

A weak winter sunset in the gardens, he watches it.
After a moment Stephen comes in with a tray, a cup of tea on it. He hands the cup up to Johnny without a word. Johnny takes it without looking at him and settles a little on the pile of things, and drinks from it neatly, gazing out over the darkening lawns.

Stephen It's six o'clock, sir. Do you want to hear the headlines?

Johnny I think so, yes. (*A glance.*) Somebody leaked to the media, Stephen.

83

Stephen I saw the Special Branch man down at the gates again, yak-yakking to the journalists. No discretion, whatsoever.

Johnny (*quietly*) Get that man in here, Stephen.

Stephen I will, Mr Silvester. One good turn deserves another. (*going to the radio*) Thank God. Any news from the doctor?

Johnny Yes. Yes. Inconclusive. (*after a long moment*) Well, I can't lie to *you*, Stephen. I will not offer you – mendacity. Tennessee Williams. (*A moment.*) The high jump.

Stephen (*genuinely*) I'm sorry to hear that.

Johnny Who knows their fate? Miracles abound. (*with evident courage*) Ultimately – well, ultimately, the King of Ultima Thule will die.

Stephen (*nodding, after a moment*) Just ourselves alone for dinner, I gather?

Johnny Ourselves alone.

Stephen I think the lamb then, sir, nice Wicklow lamb? That will give you heart.

Johnny And the lamb will lie down with the lion.

Stephen The lamb, hopefully, will be eaten by the lion, and enjoyed.

> *Johnny grunts in assent.*
> *Stephen switches on the radio, looks back at Johnny, thinks of saying something. Doesn't, goes out.*
> *The Angelus on the radio, with its tolling bell. Tolls for a while.*
> *The End.*